The New & Healthier Approach to
Deep-Fry Cuisine
Mable Hoffman

ANOTHER BEST SELLING VOLUME FROM HPBOOKS

Photography: deGennaro Associates, Mazola Corn Oil, page 55.
Food Stylist: Mable Hoffman

HPBooks
A division of Price Stern Sloan, Inc.
360 North La Cienega Boulevard
Los Angeles, California 90048

©1989 HPBooks
Printed in U.S.A.

9 8 7 6 5 4 3 2 1

The Art of Frying

The art of frying foods is one of our oldest cooking methods. When cooking was done over an open fire or in a kitchen fireplace, it was much easier to fry or boil food than to bake it. As gas and electric ranges became available, everyone continued to fry in skillets or large pans on the top of the range. Eventually, the first generation of electric deep-fryers appeared on the market. They easily produced golden brown food when properly used. However, improper use and inadequate product features often resulted in poor quality foods with inconsistent results. This was discouraging and resulted in less interest in deep-frying at home.

About that time, fast food businesses sprang up everywhere, offering a selection of popular fried foods. A generation of children grew up thinking that French fries and doughnuts always came from fast food chains instead of the home kitchen.

A new generation of fryers that consistently produce deliciously golden, light foods with sealed-in flavor are now available. And they have made deep-frying a lot easier and more efficient. They are safe and some have a lid that locks. The sealed lid keeps the spatter and cleanup inside the deep-fryer. Thermostatic controls maintain the correct temperature to ensure that the food is sealed in a coating that's always crisp and golden brown. The charcoal filter in the sealed lid of some models provides an automatic cleaning system that absorbs unpleasant frying odors.

With the return of deep-frying at home came the dreaded work "cholesterol." Everyone became more health conscious and some extremists made us feel guilty about enjoying fried foods. In the past several years, we have realized that we can enjoy deep-fried foods and still be healthy. There are three main factors to remember in nutritious meal planning that includes fried foods:

- Select low-fat meats, fish and poultry. Carefully trim edges of meat to remove any fat; remove skin from poultry. Coat fish with a thin layer of crumbs.
- Fry with healthful polyunsaturated oil, such as vegetable or corn oil, in stead of saturated fats or hydrogenated shortening. Polyunsaturated oils can withstand the proper high temperature for frying without smoking or burning.
- Proper cooking time and temperature will limit absorption of oils. Allow adequate time for your deep-fryer to heat before adding the food. Do not add too much food at one time.

By using one of the new generation of fryers with suitable features, and carefully choosing low-fat foods and polyunsaturated oils in which to fry, you can now enjoy fried foods in a nutritious and healthier approach to good eating.

MANAGING YOUR DEEP-FRYER

Deep-frying is a very fast cooking method that results in delectable flavors and crunchy textures. In order to achieve maximum quality, it is very important that foods and equipment are properly prepared before you start.

Frying is as safe as any other form of cooking if you follow a few basic principles. Start off with a quality product that will give you reliable performance. Consider the better models that have many desirable features and conveniences. The fryer should be clean and dry and placed on a level surface. Any moisture in the fryer will cause the hot oil to spatter. Prepare fryer as recommended by the manufacturer.

Here are some typical questions and the answers to make the frying process easier for you, and the fried foods more enjoyable.

Are deep-fryers safe to use?

All electrical appliances, especially those that get hot, must be used with caution. Some better deep-fryers have a safety locking lid with a hermetic rubber seal around the edge of the lid. Such fryers prevent dangerous spills of hot oil. They are much safer around children than uncovered fryers. Also, frying with the lid in the closed position prevents annoying spatters and oily film that has to be cleaned off kitchen counters and walls.

Can you eliminate annoying frying odors?

The most common complaint about deep-frying, the objectionable cooking odors, has been solved by those fryers that have a charcoal filter cartridge in the lid. The activated charcoal granules absorb odors and the grease in the vapors given off while frying. The lingering unpleasant smell of oil permeating your house is a thing of the past. The charcoal filter can easily be replaced and its effectiveness depends on how frequently and for how long the fryer is used.

What kind of oil should be used?

Choose any reliable brand of polyunsaturated cooking oil except olive oil. For other cooking, olive oil is fine, but not for deep-frying. Butter, margarine and lard are not recommended due to their high cholesterol content and because they have a fairly low smoking temperature. Cooking oils are ideal because they are colorless, almost odorless, and can be heated at high temperatures without burning. The flavor of the foods you are frying is most important, so you don't want to use a strong-flavored oil.

3

Unpleasant frying odors and greasy vapors are trapped in the charcoal filter that is easily inserted in the lid of the Tefal deep-fryer.

The built-in 20 minute timer on the Tefal deep-fryer is a convenient feature. The handy external basket control that raises and lowers the basket can be seen.

A locking lid is a desirable safety feature, especially when fryer is used near children. The viewing window in lid can be seen on this Tefal deep-fryer.

How much oil is needed for frying?

Each recipe calls for "oil for frying." It is not possible to give the exact amount because the quantity required varies with the brand of fryer. Be sure to follow the manufacturer's recommendation for the exact quantity because the most efficient amount for the unit has been pre-determined by the manufacturer. Pour the oil to the line indicated inside the fryer. If you do not use enough oil, food will not cook properly. If you use too much, it may bubble over the top, creating a mess.

What is the correct frying temperature?

Most fryers will heat oil to a temperature of 370°F to 380°F (188°C to 194°C) which is the proper range for almost all deep-frying. Some models are equipped with a lower temperature setting of about 340°F (170°C). Delicate foods such as mushrooms and some fish products are at their best when cooked at a lower temperature. Also, some foods may be partially cooked at a lower temperature, then finished at a higher temperature just before serving.

It takes about ten to fifteen minutes for oil to reach the proper temperature. Some fryers have a "ready light" that goes out indicating that the oil is hot and that food can be added. The thermostatic control built into each fryer cycles the heat on and off to maintain a fairly uniform temperature while frying. This ensures appetizing food that is sealed in a crisp, dry coating that is not soggy or scorched.

Is there a special way to prepare foods for frying?

Have the food ready when the oil is hot. Cut it in uniform pieces for proper cooking and even browning. If the food is moist, pat it dry with paper towels before putting it into the fryer. Any water on the food will spatter when dropped into hot oil. Also, if wet foods are coated with flour or crumbs, they will be soggy instead of crisp or crunchy. Wet foods such as potatoes soaked in water or meats that are marinated should be drained then patted dry with paper towels before they are fried. For coated foods, let excess batter drip off; lightly shake off any loose crumbs.

Why are different kinds of coating used?

Coatings serve several purposes. For example, the coating on croquettes holds in the natural moisture of the food and keeps it from direct contact with the hot oil while forming a crisp outer covering that's so good to eat. Whatever coating you use, be sure to cover the surface evenly so it will turn a beautiful, crusty golden brown. Some foods, such as doughnuts, do not require a coating. The egg-flour-sugar combination browns easily, creating its own golden brown covering when fried.

What is the best way to put food in the deep-fryer?

The better deep-fryers have an external control that lets you raise and lower the frying basket without opening the lid. This is a very desirable feature. Most foods may be put into the raised basket which is then lowered into the hot oil while the lid is closed.

Place food in the basket with a long-handled metal spoon, tongs or pancake turner. A fork is not recommended for handling food to be fried. It makes holes which allow juices to escape from the food and allows oil to enter the food making it greasy. Be careful not to overload the basket. Too much food will lower the temperature of the oil, causing the food to absorb too much oil and produce a dry interior because of additional cooking time. In the case of batter-type foods that are dropped into hot oil by spoonfuls, it is better to lower the basket into the hot oil first, then add the food.

How important is timing the frying process?

Correct cooking time is very important for consistently perfect results. Keeping food in the hot oil excessively long may result in over-cooking and burning. It can alter the food's taste and make it greasy. The handy minute timer built into some models of deep-fryers lets you select the desired frying time for each recipe. A bell rings to remind you when the food is done. You can, of course, use a kitchen timer or wall clock.

Deep-fryers with a window in the lid are handy for viewing the food as it is being cooked. You can see how brown **the food is without opening the lid. But** you will soon learn to depend on proper timing rather than watching the food.

What do you do when food is done?

When food is done, raise the basket and allow food to drain for several sec-onds. If there is a locked lid, unlock it; allow steam to escape before you raise the lid fully. Be careful not to touch hot metal parts. Use the handle to remove the basket with cooked food. Then drain on three or four thicknesses of paper towels before serving.

Can the oil be re-used?

With normal use and proper filtering, you should be able to use the same oil over and over many times. It's difficult to state the exact number of times that the oil can be used. Foods with a high sugar content, crumbs that fall into the hot oil, and strong flavors reduce the number of times you can use it.

Some models provide optional paper oil strainers that make it easy to strain the oil of crumbs and bits of batter. The strained oil can be stored in the fryer, especially those fryers with a locking lid. If you aren't planning to use the fryer for quite awhile, oil keeps better in a covered jar in the refrigerator.

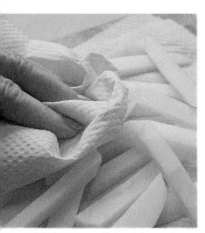

Make sure all food is as dry as possible before frying. If food, such as potatoes, has been soaked in water, drain well, then pat dry with paper towels.

Be sure to drain fried foods carefully as soon as they come out of the deep-fryer. Several layers of paper towels on a baking sheet will do the job.

Do not crowd food in the deep-fryer. Give it enough space to move around without sticking together. Use a metal spatula to turn food over.

Appetizers

Could you use extra help when getting ready for a party? Let your deep-fryer come to the rescue. It can give you hot, crunchy appetizers in minutes.

Do all of your advance preparation early in the day. Combine ingredients for the appetizers you're planning to fry. Then fry them just before guests arrive; drain and serve while still warm and crispy.

Even better, arrange uncooked ingredients on a tray and let guests fry their own appetizers. Everyone will love the idea of having a part in the preparation, and also enjoy choosing favorite appetizers. Fryers that have locking lids can be brought to the table because there is no spatter or objectionable odor.

Start with suggestions from this book. Then vary the fillings or coatings to create your own recipes. For example, I have included several won ton appetizers because they are so versatile. They are great when you want to have a special appetizer. Won ton skins or wrappers may be found in oriental markets and gourmet shops, and in the frozen or deli sections of many supermarkets. They freeze well, so pick up a package the next time you see them in the market; freeze and keep on hand until you need them. They are already cut in squares. Just thaw them the day you want to serve them; mix up your favorite filling, fill and fry. No doubt you have seen several ways to fold won tons. I have included directions for one of the traditional folds, in addition to a very simple triangle.

Be careful not to overcook appetizers. They are small and usually take less time than most main dishes or larger portions of food. When possible, fry a few appetizers at a time, and serve right away.

Fried Camembert, page 8.

Fried Camembert

Serve on fresh spinach leaves for a unique presentation. (Photo on page 7.)

3 tablespoons butter
1 heaping tablespoon all-purpose flour
1 cup milk

2 tablespoons semolina or rice flour
Salt and pepper to taste
4 oz. Camembert cheese, cubed

Coating:
1 egg, beaten
Dash cayenne pepper

1 cup all-purpose flour
1 cup dried bread crumbs

▬▬▬▬▬▬ In a small saucepan, melt butter. Stir in flour until well blended. Stir in milk, then semolina or rice flour. Season with salt and pepper. Bring to a boil, stirring constantly, and cook until mixture is very thick. Add cubed cheese and cook, stirring constantly, until cheese is melted. Spread cheese mixture in an 8″ x 8″ dish. Refrigerate at least 2 hours. Cut cheese mixture in 2-inch squares. In a small bowl, combine beaten egg and cayenne pepper. Dip squares into flour, then into beaten egg and then into bread crumbs. If necessary, repeat to coat evenly. Place several squares into raised fryer basket. Lower into hot oil and fry until golden brown on both sides. Drain and serve warm. Makes 16 appetizers.

Cheese Turnovers

Choose your favorite kind of cheese!

2 cups all-purpose flour
½ teaspoon salt
1 teaspoon baking powder
1 teaspoon chili powder

½ cup milk
1 egg
¼ cup butter or margarine, melted
Vegetable oil for frying

Cheese Filling:
2 tablespoons green onion
   thinly sliced
2 tablespoons chopped fresh parsley
½ tablespoon butter or margarine
⅛ teaspoon salt

⅛ teaspoon pepper
2 cups shredded Cheddar or
   Monterey Jack cheese (8 oz.)

▬▬▬▬▬▬ In a medium bowl, mix flour, ½ teaspoon salt, baking powder and chili powder. In a small bowl, beat milk and egg. Stir into flour mixture. Stir in melted butter or margarine; dough will be soft. Turn dough onto a lightly floured board. Knead about 4 minutes until smooth. Shape in a ball. Place in a bowl, cover and chill 30 minutes. Prepare Cheese Filling. Divide dough in half. On a lightly floured board, roll out each half of dough about ⅛-inch thick. Cut in 3-inch circles. Place about 1 teaspoon of Cheese Filling in center of each circle. Moisten edges, fold dough over Cheese Filling and press edges with fork to seal securely. Place several turnovers into raised fryer basket. Lower into hot oil and fry about 1 minute or until brown on both sides. Drain and serve warm. Makes about 14 appetizers.

Cheese Filling:
Cook onion and parsley in ½ tablespoon butter or margarine until onion is tender. Remove from heat. Stir in salt, pepper and shredded Cheddar or Monterey Jack cheese.

Shortcut Nachos

Fry extra tortilla wedges for use as snacks or with your favorite dips.

4 flour tortillas
Vegetable oil for frying
2 cups shredded Monterey Jack or
   Cheddar cheese (8 oz.)

¼ cup canned chopped green chili
   peppers

■■■■■■■■■ Cut each tortilla in 8 wedges. Place fryer basket in lowered position. Drop several pieces at a time into hot oil. Fry about 30 seconds on each side or until light brown and puffy. Drain. Sprinkle immediately with shredded Monterey Jack or Cheddar cheese and chopped peppers. Serve warm. Fry tortillas ahead of time, if desired; then at serving time, sprinkle with cheese and peppers and place in oven broiler until cheese melts. Makes 32 appetizers.

Oriental Appetizer Balls

So good you'll want to double the recipe for a party.

¼ lb. ground pork sausage
¼ lb. cooked shrimp, finely chopped
¼ cup finely chopped water chestnuts
¼ cup finely chopped onion

2 tablespoons soy sauce
⅛ teaspoon sugar
1 egg, slightly beaten
Vegetable oil for frying

■■■■■■■■■ In a medium bowl, combine ground sausage with shrimp, water chestnuts, onion, soy sauce, sugar and egg. Shape in 1-inch balls. Place fryer basket in lowered position. Drop balls into hot oil. Fry until brown. Drain and serve hot. Makes about 30 appetizers.

Hot Dog Puffs

Like bite-size corn dogs!

1 egg
½ cup milk
1 teaspoon prepared mustard
1 cup all-purpose flour
1 teaspoon baking powder

½ teaspoon salt
5 frankfurters
Vegetable oil for frying
Relish, ketchup or prepared mustard,
   if desired

■■■■■■■■■ In a medium bowl, mix egg, milk and mustard. Stir in flour, baking powder and salt. Mix until smooth. Cut each frankfurter in 8 to 10 slices. Add to batter. Place fryer basket in lowered position. Drop batter by tablespoonfuls into hot oil. Fry about 2½ to 3 minutes or until golden brown. Drain and serve hot with relish, ketchup or mustard, if desired. Makes 10 puffs.

Mini Mandarin Drumsticks

Bake on the spicy glaze just before your guests arrive. (Photo on page 13.)

12 chicken wings
½ cup cornstarch
1 egg, slightly beaten
¼ teaspoon salt

¼ teaspoon seasoned salt
2 tablespoons milk
Vegetable oil for frying
Sesame seeds

Spicy Glaze:
1 cup sugar
¼ cup water
½ cup vinegar

1 teaspoon soy sauce
1 tablespoon ketchup
1 tablespoon chopped green onion

▬▬▬▬▬ Cut chicken wings at joints; discard wing tips. Scrape and push meat to one end of bone so each piece resembles a small drumstick. In a medium bowl, combine cornstarch, egg, salt, seasoned salt and milk. Mix until smooth. Dip each drumstick into batter. Place several drumsticks into raised fryer basket. Lower into hot oil and fry 3 minutes or until lightly browned; drain. Chill or freeze until needed, if desired. Prepare Spicy Glaze. Dip fried drumsticks into Spicy Glaze. In a shallow baking pan, arrange in a single layer. Bake at 350°F (175°C) 30 minutes, basting several times with Spicy Glaze. Sprinkle with sesame seeds and serve hot. Makes 24 appetizers.

Spicy Glaze:
In a small saucepan, combine all ingredients. Bring to a boil, stirring until sugar dissolves.

Fried Cheese Balls

Great cheese flavor!

1 egg, slightly beaten
¼ teaspoon baking powder
1 tablespoon all-purpose flour
1 cup shredded sharp Cheddar cheese
   (4 oz.)

2 tablespoons chopped ripe olives
¼ teaspoon seasoned salt
Vegetable oil for frying

▬▬▬▬▬ In a medium bowl, combine egg, baking powder, flour, shredded Cheddar cheese, olives and seasoned salt. Place fryer basket in lowered position. Drop batter by teaspoonfuls into hot oil. Fry about 1½ to 2 minutes or until golden. Drain and serve hot. Makes about 15 appetizers.

*Cut chicken wings at joints to make three pieces.
Discard wing tips.*

*With a sharp knife, push meat to one end of the bone so
it resembles a small drumstick.*

How to Make
Mini Mandarin Drumsticks

*After dipping drumstick in batter, drop into hot oil.
If using plastic tongs, be careful to prevent plastic
from touching hot oil. Metal utensils are preferred.*

*Dip fried chicken into sauce, then brush with sauce
several times while baking.*

South of the Border Won Ton

A tasty change from the traditional won ton filling! These are good plain or with guacamole sauce.

½ lb. lean ground beef
1 green onion, finely chopped
½ teaspoon salt
½ teaspoon chili powder
¼ teaspoon garlic salt

½ cup shredded Monterey Jack cheese
  (2 oz.)
2 tablespoons chopped ripe olives
30 to 35 won ton skins or wrappers
Vegetable oil for frying

███████████ In a small skillet, break up beef with a fork. Cook with onion, salt, chili powder and garlic salt several minutes. Stir in shredded Monterey Jack cheese and olives. Cool slightly. Place about 1 rounded teaspoon of filling in center of each won ton skin. Moisten edges of skin. Fold 2 opposite corners together, forming a triangle. Seal edges. Place several won ton into raised fryer basket. Lower into hot oil and fry about 1 minute or until crisp and golden. Drain and serve hot. Makes 30 to 35 appetizers.

French-Fried Mushrooms

Terrific as an appetizer or with roast beef.

1 egg
½ cup milk
½ teaspoon salt
30 medium mushrooms
⅓ cup all-purpose flour
1 cup corn flake crumbs

Vegetable oil for frying
Salt to taste
Grated Parmesan cheese
Lemon wedges, if desired

███████████ In a shallow dish, beat egg with milk and ½ teaspoon salt. In another dish, roll mushrooms in flour. Dip mushrooms into egg mixture and coat with corn flake crumbs. Place several mushrooms into raised fryer basket. Lower into hot oil and fry 1 to 2 minutes or until golden. Drain and sprinkle with salt to taste and grated Parmesan cheese. Serve with lemon wedges, if desired. Makes 30 appetizers.

Clockwise from top: French-Fried Mushrooms, above; Mini Mandarin Drumsticks, page 10; South-of-the-Border Won Ton, above.

Fiesta Chips

Pie-shaped puffs can be served as dippers or as a bread.

½ cup all-purpose flour
⅓ cup yellow cornmeal
1 teaspoon salt
½ teaspoon chili powder

⅓ cup water
Vegetable oil for frying
Avocado or bean dip, if desired

In a small bowl, mix flour, cornmeal, salt and chili powder. Add water gradually, stirring until flour mixture is moistened. Turn onto a lightly floured board. Knead about 3 minutes or until smooth. Shape dough in a ball. Place in a bowl and cover. Chill 30 minutes. Divide dough in half. Roll each half in an 8-inch circle. Cut each circle in 8 triangles. Place fryer basket in lowered position. Fry triangles in hot oil until golden brown. Drain and serve warm or cool. Serve with avocado or bean dip, if desired. Makes 16 appetizers.

Clam Puffs

Start your party right with clam appetizers.

1 egg
¼ cup milk
⅔ cup all-purpose flour
½ teaspoon baking powder
¼ teaspoon salt
⅛ teaspoon cayenne pepper

1 (6½-oz.) can minced clams,
   well-drained
2 tablespoons minced green onions
1 teaspoon minced fresh parsley
Vegetable oil for frying

In a medium bowl, beat egg with milk. Add flour, baking powder, salt and cayenne pepper. Beat until well-blended. Stir in clams, onions and parsley. Place fryer basket in lowered position. Drop by teaspoonfuls into hot oil. Fry 2 to 2½ minutes or until golden brown. Drain and serve warm. Makes about 18 to 20 appetizers.

Spiced Walnuts

Bet you can't stop eating these!

1 teaspoon salt
½ teaspoon ground cinnamon
¼ teaspoon ground nutmeg
¼ teaspoon ground cloves

¼ teaspoon allspice
½ cup sugar
2 cups walnut halves
Vegetable oil for frying

In a paper bag, combine salt, spices and sugar. Using fryer basket, fry 1 cup of nuts at a time in hot oil until golden brown. Drain. While warm, drop into paper bag and shake bag to coat nuts well. Makes 2 cups.

Fried Nuts

Try a different flavor each time.

2 cups peanuts, pecan halves or whole blanched almonds

Vegetable oil for frying
1 teaspoon salt or seasoned salt

━━━━━━━━━ Using fryer basket, fry 1 cup of nuts at a time in hot oil 1 to 1½ minutes or until golden brown. Drain and sprinkle with salt or seasoned salt. Serve warm or cool. Makes 2 cups.

Variations:
Sprinkle 1 teaspoon chili powder over peanuts.
Sprinkle 2 teaspoons soy sauce over pecans.
Sprinkle 1 teaspoon curry powder over almonds.

Fried Nuts, above.

Cheese Puffs

A delightful finger food!

1 sheet frozen puff pastry, thawed
Vegetable oil for frying

Cheese Filling:
1 cup shredded Montery Jack
cheese (4 oz.)
1 tablespoon chopped cilantro

½ tablespoon butter or margarine
Salt and pepper to taste

▬▬▬▬▬ Prepare Cheese Filling. Place puff pastry on a lightly floured board. Cut out 3-inch circles. Place about 2 tablespoonfuls of filling in center of each circle. Moisten edges of circles and fold pastry over filling. Press edges to seal securely. Place several in raised fryer basket. Lower into hot oil and fry until golden. Drain and serve warm. Makes about 12 appetizers.

Cheese Filling:
In a small bowl, combine all ingredients.

Fried Cheese Sticks

The outside will be golden and crunchy; the cheese inside will be partially melted.

8 oz. Swiss or Monterey Jack cheese
2 tablespoons all-purpose flour
1 egg, beaten slightly

1 cup crushed sesame crackers
(about 24)
Vegetable oil for frying

▬▬▬▬▬ Cut cheese in sticks about 3 inches long and ¾ inch thick. Dip sticks into flour, then into egg. Gently roll sticks in crumbs, pressing lightly on all sides. Dip again into egg, then into crumbs. Refrigerate about 1 hour. Place fryer basket in lowered position. Fry in hot oil 1 to 1½ minutes or until outside is golden brown. Drain and serve immediately. Makes 8 sticks.

Cheese Puffs, above.

Fried Won Ton

Try a Chinese tradition.

½ lb. uncooked boneless pork, chicken
  or turkey
2 tablespoons vegetable oil
2 tablespoons chopped green onions
4 canned water chestnuts, chopped
1 tablespoon sherry wine

¼ teaspoon salt
2 teaspoons cornstarch
2 tablespoons soy sauce
25 to 35 won ton skins or wrappers
Vegetable oil for frying

■■■■■■■ Finely chop uncooked pork, chicken or turkey. In a medium skillet, cook meat in 2 tablespoons oil several minutes. Stir in onions, water chestnuts, wine and salt. Dissolve cornstarch in soy sauce. Add to mixture in skillet. Cook, stirring constantly, over low heat until thick and translucent. Place 1 rounded teaspoon of filling in center of each won ton skin. Moisten edges of skin. Fold 2 opposite corners together, forming a triangle. Seal edges. Pull right and left corners of folded triangle down and below folded edge so they slightly overlap. Moisten overlapping corners and pinch together. Place several won ton into raised fryer basket. Lower into hot oil and fry 1 to 1½ minutes or until crisp and golden. Drain and serve hot. Makes 25 to 35 appetizers.

Crab Won Ton

Add gourmet flavor to your meal!

¼ lb. cooked crab meat
1 (3-oz.) pkg. cream cheese, room
  temperature
1 tablespoon soft bread crumbs

¼ teaspoon sesame seeds
¼ teaspoon seasoned salt
20 to 25 won ton skins or wrappers
Vegetable oil for frying

Chinese Mustard Sauce:
2 tablespoons dry mustard
2 tablespoons water

■■■■■■■ Prepare Chinese Mustard Sauce. Drain and flake crab meat. Pat with paper towels to remove as much moisture as possible. In a medium bowl, combine cream cheese, bread crumbs, sesame seeds and seasoned salt. Stir in crab meat. Place about 1 teaspoon of crab mixture in center of each won ton skin. Moisten edges of skin. Fold 2 opposite corners together, forming a triangle. Seal edges. Pull right and left corners of folded triangle down and below folded edge so they slightly overlap. Moisten overlapping corners and pinch together. Place several won ton into raised fryer basket. Lower into hot oil and fry about 1 minute or until crisp and golden. Drain and serve with Chinese Mustard Sauce. Makes about 20 to 25 appetizers.

Chinese Mustard Sauce:
In a small bowl, combine dry mustard and water. Stir until well-blended.

Place filling in center of won ton skin. Brush edges of won ton skin with water.

How to Fold Won Ton

Fold two opposite corners together, forming a triangle. Press edges to seal.

Pull the right and left corners of folded triangle down and below folded edge so they overlap slightly. Moisten and pinch together.

Tuna Won Ton

Tempt their tastes with tuna.

1 (6½-oz.) can tuna, drained
8 water chestnuts, finely chopped
2 green onions, chopped
1 tablespoon soy sauce

½ teaspoon sugar
1 egg, beaten
30 to 35 won ton skins or wrappers
Vegetable oil for frying

▬▬▬▬▬▬ In a medium bowl, flake tuna. Combine with water chestnuts, onions, soy sauce, sugar and egg. Place about 1 teaspoon of tuna mixture in center of each won ton skin. Moisten edges of skin. Fold 2 opposite corners together, forming a triangle. Seal edges. Pull right and left corners of folded triangle down and below folded edge so they slightly overlap. Moisten overlapping corners and pinch together. Using fryer basket, fry 5 or 6 at a time in hot oil about 1 minute or until crisp and golden. Drain and serve hot. Makes 30 to 35 appetizers.

Fried Ravioli

A savory filling encased in delicious pastry!

1 egg, beaten
1 tablespoon water
½ teaspoon salt

1½ teaspoons vegetable oil
⅔ cup all-purpose flour
Vegetable oil for frying

Filling:
½ lb. cooked ground beef
1 egg, beaten
¼ cup chopped green onion

2 tablespoons grated Parmesan cheese
Salt and pepper to taste

▬▬▬▬▬▬ Prepare filling and refrigerate until needed. In a medium bowl, combine egg, water, salt and 1½ teaspoons oil. Add flour and mix to form a ball. Turn onto a lightly floured board and knead until smooth, about 10 minutes. Cover and let stand 1 hour. Divide dough in 2 equal pieces. On lightly floured board, roll out 1 piece of dough paper-thin. Place teaspoonfuls of filling about 1 inch apart on ½ of dough, leaving 1 inch on all outside edges. Pull remaining side of dough over filling. Press down dough with fingers between individual fillings. With a knife, cut out ravioli halfway between fillings, leaving enough dough on all sides to prevent filling from falling out. Repeat with remaining piece of dough and filling. Cover ravioli and let stand 45 minutes. Place several in raised fryer basket. Lower into hot oil and fry until golden brown. Drain and serve hot. Makes about 2 dozen.

Filling:
In a small bowl, combine all ingredients.

Fried Ravioli, above.

Miniature Chilies Rellenos

Puffy batter around cheese and chilies.

1 (4-oz.) can whole green chilies
¼ lb. Monterey Jack cheese
3 tablespoons all-purpose flour
2 eggs, separated

⅛ teaspoon salt
Vegetable oil for frying
Salsa or taco sauce, if desired

■■■■■■■ Drain chilies and discard seeds. Cut in 12 strips. Cut Monterey Jack cheese in 12 cubes. Wrap a chili strip around each cheese cube. Roll in 1 tablespoon of flour. In a medium bowl, beat egg whites until soft peaks form. In a small bowl, beat egg yolks and salt until thick. Stir remaining 2 tablespoons of flour into beaten yolks. Fold yolk mixture into beaten egg whites. Coat each chili-cheese cube with egg mixture. Using fryer basket, fry 5 cubes at a time in hot oil about 5 minutes or until done. Drain and serve hot. Serve with salsa or taco sauce, if desired. Makes 12 appetizers.

Green Cheese Balls

A super spinach idea.

1 (10-oz.) pkg. frozen spinach, thawed
2 eggs, slightly beaten
1½ cups fine dry bread crumbs
½ teaspoon salt
½ teaspoon seasoned salt

1 teaspoon grated onion
½ cup shredded Cheddar cheese (2 oz.)
Dash ground nutmeg
Vegetable oil for frying
Hollandaise or tomato sauce, if desired

■■■■■■■ Drain and squeeze spinach to remove all water. Finely chop spinach and place in a large bowl. Add eggs, bread crumbs, salt, seasoned salt, onion, shredded Cheddar cheese and nutmeg. Shape in ¾- to 1-inch balls. Place fryer basket in lowered position. Drop balls into hot oil. Fry until brown. Drain and serve hot. Serve with Hollandaise or tomato sauce, if desired. Makes 20 to 25 appetizers.

Chicken Taquitos

A popular Mexican-style dish that you can make in your own deep-fryer.

2 whole chicken breasts
1 cup chicken broth
¼ teaspoon salt

¼ cup chopped canned green chilies,
    drained
12 corn tortillas
Guacamole

■■■■■■■ In a large saucepan, combine chicken, broth and salt. Bring to a boil. Cover and simmer 20 to 25 minutes or until chicken is tender. Drain; cool slightly. Remove skin and bones from chicken. Pull chicken apart in small shreds. Combine with green chilies. Place about 3 tablespoons of chicken mixture in a narrow strip along 1 side of each tortilla. Roll up tightly; secure with a wooden pick. Place several in raised fryer basket. Lower into hot oil and fry 1½ to 2 minutes or until golden brown. Drain. Dip into guacamole. Makes 12 appetizers.

Dallas Dippers

Giant puffy disks with a super South-of-the-Border flavor. Serve as snacks or as dippers for guacamole or your favorite dip.

2 cups buttermilk baking mix
½ cup cold water
1 teaspoon chili powder

Cornmeal
Vegetable oil for frying

In a medium bowl, combine baking mix, water and chili powder to form soft dough. On a lightly floured board, knead 5 times. Divide in 16 equal parts. Shape each in a ball on a board sprinkled with cornmeal. Roll each ball in a 4-inch circle. Place fryer basket in lowered position. Drop circles into hot oil. Fry until puffy and golden. Drain and serve warm or cool. Makes 16 appetizers.

Mini Chicken-Almond Turnovers

Rich and flaky pastry with delicious chicken filling.

1 cup all-purpose flour
½ teaspoon salt

⅔ cup whipping cream
Vegetable oil for frying

Chicken-Almond Filling:
1 (4¾-oz.) can chicken spread
2 tablespoons chopped blanched almonds

1 hard-cooked egg, peeled, chopped
1 tablespoon imitation bacon bits

Prepare Chicken-Almond Filling. In a medium bowl, combine flour and salt. Stir in cream to make stiff dough. On lightly floured board, roll out dough about ⅛ inch thick. Cut in 2-inch circles. Place about 1 teaspoon of Chicken-Almond Filling in center of each circle. Fold over and press edges together. Place several turnovers into raised fryer basket. Lower into hot oil and fry about 1½ to 2 minutes or until golden brown. Drain and serve warm or cool. Makes 30 appetizers.

Chicken-Almond Filling:
In a small bowl, combine chicken spread, almonds, egg and bacon bits. Blend well.

Doughnuts

Doughnuts are favorites, everywhere! They are a form of deep-fried cake or bread. Cake doughnuts are made of flour, milk, eggs and seasonings with a leavening agent of baking powder and/or baking soda. The leavening ingredients, in addition to the eggs, make doughnuts puff up when they are in hot oil. Bread doughnuts are made with yeast. This kind takes longer to make because you have to wait for the yeast to "work."

Naturally, most of the recipes in this section are doughnuts with the typical round shape and a hole in the center. However, some that use the traditional ingredients are dropped from a spoon rather than rolled and cut out. When making drop doughnuts, try to make the approximate size indicated in the recipe. If they are too large, the outside browns too much before the center is done.

Don't be afraid to try even if you've never made doughnuts before. Read through the recipe, making sure you have all ingredients on hand. Then follow the directions, being careful to measure accurately. I find that the flour measurement is most accurate when I spoon the flour from the canister (or from the bag of flour) into a measuring cup. Then level off the cup with a spatula. For most cake-type doughnuts, it is easier to roll out the dough if you chill it for an hour or two ahead of time. After rolling out the dough and cutting out the doughnuts, let them stand 10 to 15 minutes, if possible, while heating the oil in the deep-fryer. Then carefully lift each doughnut with a pancake turner, place it in the raised fryer basket and gently lower it into the hot oil. Fry it the approximate time indicated in the recipe.

For yeast doughnuts, most recipes allow a slight variation in the amount of flour. Use the amount that makes the dough easy for you to handle. Follow the suggested times for the dough to double, but check it occasionally. When the yeast doughnuts are ready to be fried. lift them carefully to keep their nice round shape.

For glazed doughnuts, it's a good idea to dip them into the glaze while they're still warm. For sugar-coating, wait until they're almost cool before dipping them or shaking them in a plastic bag.

Old-Fashioned Doughnuts, page 28.

Spiced Raisin Balls

A quick, spicy doughnut filled with raisins and pecans.

2 cups all-purpose flour
¼ cup sugar
1 tablespoon baking powder
1 teaspoon ground cinnamon
¼ teaspoon ground cloves
½ teaspoon salt
1 egg, beaten

¾ cup milk
¼ cup vegetable oil
¼ cup coarsely chopped pecans
¼ cup dark raisins
Vegetable oil for frying
Sugar, if desired

━━━━━ In a large bowl, stir together flour, ¼ cup sugar, baking powder, cinnamon, cloves and salt. In a medium bowl, combine egg, milk and ¼ cup oil. Stir into dry ingredients until moistened. Stir in pecans and raisins. Place fryer basket in lowered position. Drop by teaspoonfuls into hot oil. Fry about 2½ to 3 minutes or until brown. Drain and roll in sugar, if desired. Makes 25 to 30 balls.

Buttermilk Doughnuts

Delicious plain, sprinkled with sugar or glazed.

1 egg
½ cup sugar
½ cup buttermilk
½ teaspoon vanilla extract
2 cups all-purpose flour
1½ teaspoons baking powder

¼ teaspoon baking soda
¼ teaspoon salt
¼ teaspoon ground ginger
½ teaspoon ground mace
Vegetable oil for frying

Glaze:
½ cup sifted powdered sugar
1 tablespoon warm milk

━━━━━ In a medium bowl, beat egg until light and foamy. Beat in sugar. Add buttermilk and vanilla. Mix in flour, baking powder, baking soda, salt, ginger and mace. Chill about 1 hour. Prepare Glaze. On a lightly floured board, pat out dough ¾-inch thick. Cut with lightly floured doughnut cutter. Place several doughnuts into raised fryer basket. Lower into hot oil and fry about 2 to 2½ minutes or until golden brown. Drain and dip top of warm doughnuts into glaze. Place doughnuts glaze-side-up on a rack. Makes 8 or 9 doughnuts.

Glaze:
In a small bowl, combine powdered sugar and warm milk. Blend until smooth.

Old-Fashioned Potato Doughnuts

Moist and flavorful on the inside, crunchy on the outside.

1½ cups all-purpose flour
⅓ cup sugar
1 tablespoon baking powder
¼ teaspoon ground nutmeg
¼ teaspoon salt
½ cup prepared mashed potatoes

2 tablespoons butter or margarine
1 egg
2 tablespoons milk
½ teaspoon vanilla extract
Vegetable oil for frying
Sifted powdered sugar

████████ In a medium bowl, combine flour, sugar, baking powder, nutmeg and salt. With a pastry blender or fork, cut in mashed potatoes and butter or margarine until mixture resembles coarse crumbs. In a small bowl, mix egg, milk and vanilla. Stir into flour mixture. Knead on a lightly floured board until smooth. Roll out dough about ½-inch thick. Cut with a floured doughnut cutter. Place several doughnuts into raised fryer basket. Lower into hot oil and fry about 2 minutes or until golden brown. Drain and cool. Sprinkle with powdered sugar. Makes 8 or 9 doughnuts.

Chocolate-Cinnamon Doughnuts

For those whose favorite flavor is chocolate.

⅔ cup sugar
1 egg beaten
2 tablespoons butter or margarine,
    softened
½ teaspoon vanilla extract
2 cups all-purpose flour
3 tablespoons unsweetened cocoa
    powder

2 teaspoons baking powder
⅛ teaspoon baking soda
½ teaspoon ground cinnamon
½ teaspoon salt
⅓ cup buttermilk
Vegetable oil for frying

Cocoa Glaze:
1 cup sifted powdered sugar
1 tablespoon unsweetened cocoa powder

½ tablespoon butter, softened
1½ tablespoons boiling water

████████ In a large bowl, gradually add sugar to egg, beating until thick and lemon-colored. Stir in softened butter or margarine and vanilla. In a medium bowl, combine flour, cocoa powder, baking powder, baking soda, cinnamon and salt. Stir into egg mixture alternately with buttermilk. Chill about 2 hours; dough will be slightly sticky. Prepare Cocoa Glaze. On a lightly floured board, roll out ½ of dough at a time about ½-inch thick. Keep remaining dough chilled. Cut with a floured doughnut cutter. Repeat with remaining dough. Place several doughnuts into raised fryer basket. Lower into hot oil and fry about 2 minutes. Drain and dip top of warm doughnuts into Cocoa Glaze. Makes 8 to 10 doughnuts.

Cocoa Glaze:
In a small bowl, combine powdered sugar, cocoa powder, softened butter and boiling water. Stir until smooth.

Old-Fashioned Doughnuts

Dress up this basic cake doughnut recipe with your favorite frosting. (Photo on page 25.)

1 egg
½ cup sugar
2 cups all-purpose flour
2 teaspoons baking powder
½ teaspoon salt

1 tablespoon melted butter
⅓ cup milk
½ teaspoon vanilla extract
Vegetable oil for frying
Additional sugar or frosting, if desired

In a large bowl, beat egg until light and lemon-colored. Gradually beat in ½ cup sugar until thick. In a medium bowl, combine flour, baking powder and salt. Add dry ingredients alternately with melted butter, milk and vanilla to egg mixture. Stir until flour is moistened. If dough is hard to handle, chill 1 hour. On a lightly floured board, roll out dough about ½-inch thick. Cut with a floured doughnut cutter. Place several doughnuts into raised fryer basket. Lower into hot oil and fry about 1 minute on each side or until golden brown. Drain and sprinkle with additional sugar or frost, if desired. Makes 8 to 10 doughnuts.

Harvest Doughnuts

Apple butter provides the spicy flavor.

2 cups buttermilk baking mix
2 tablespoons sugar
1 egg, beaten
½ cup apple butter

1 teaspoon vanilla extract
Vegetable oil for frying
½ cup chopped walnuts

Apple Butter Glaze:
1½ cups sifted powdered sugar
2 tablespoons milk

1½ tablespoons apple butter

In a large bowl, combine baking mix and sugar. In a small bowl, mix egg, apple butter and vanilla. Add to dry ingredients. Mix until smooth. Cover and chill thoroughly. Prepare Apple-Butter Glaze. On a lightly floured board, knead dough 8 to 10 times. Roll out dough about ¼-inch thick. Cut with a floured doughnut cutter. Place several doughnuts into raised fryer basket. Lower into hot oil and fry 2 minutes or until brown. Drain and dip warm doughnuts into Apple-Butter Glaze, then in walnuts. Makes 8 to 10 doughnuts.

Apple-Butter Glaze:
In a small bowl, combine powdered sugar, milk and apple butter. Mix well.

Calas

Our version of the famous New Orleans rice doughnut.

1 egg
¼ cup sugar
2 cups cold *cooked* short or medium
   grain white rice
½ cup all-purpose flour
1½ teaspoons baking powder

¼ teaspoon salt
½ teaspoon ground cinnamon
¼ teaspoon ground cloves
¼ teaspoon ground nutmeg
Vegetable oil for frying
Sifted powdered sugar

In a large bowl, beat egg and sugar until light and thick. Mix in cooked rice, flour, baking powder, salt, cinnamon, cloves and nutmeg. Place fryer basket in lowered position. Drop by teaspoonfuls into hot oil. Fry about 2 minutes or until golden. Drain and sprinkle with powdered sugar. Serve hot. Makes 20 to 24 calas.

Double-Orange Doughnuts

For those who love that real orange flavor!

3¼ cups all-purpose flour
2 teaspoons baking powder
2 eggs, beaten
⅔ cup sugar
1 teaspoon vanilla extract

1 teaspoon grated orange peel
⅔ cup orange juice
¼ cup butter or margarine, melted
Vegetable oil for frying

Orange Glaze:
2 cups sifted powdered sugar
1 teaspoon grated orange peel

3 tablespoons orange juice

In a medium bowl, combine flour and baking powder. In a large bowl, beat eggs, sugar and vanilla until thick and lemon-colored. In a small bowl, combine grated orange peel, orange juice and melted butter or margarine. Add orange mixture and ¾ of dry ingredients alternately to egg mixture. Beat with an electric mixer just until blended after each addition. Stir in remaining dry ingredients by hand. Cover and chill dough 2 hours. Prepare Orange Glaze. On a lightly floured board, roll out dough about ⅜-inch thick. Cut with a floured doughnut cutter. Place several doughnuts into raised fryer basket. Lower into hot oil and fry about 1 minute on each side or until golden. Drain and drizzle with Orange Glaze while warm. Makes 16 doughnuts.

Orange Glaze:
In a small bowl, combine powdered sugar, grated orange peel and orange juice. Stir until well blended.

Spicy Orange Puffs

So spicy and crunchy!

2 cups all-purpose flour
¼ cup sugar
1 tablespoon baking powder
½ teaspoon salt
½ teaspoon ground nutmeg
¼ cup vegetable oil
½ cup milk

¼ cup orange juice
½ teaspoon grated orange peel
1 egg, slightly beaten
Vegetable oil for frying
⅓ cup sugar
½ teaspoon ground cinnamon

▬▬▬▬▬▬ In a medium bowl, combine flour, ¼ cup sugar, baking powder, salt and nutmeg. Make a well in center. Pour in ¼ cup oil, milk, orange juice, grated orange peel and egg. Stir until well mixed. Place fryer basket in lowered position. Drop slightly rounded teaspoonfuls of batter into hot oil. Use another teaspoon to push batter off spoon. Larger puffs do not cook well in center. Fry about 2½ to 3 minutes or until brown. Drain. Mix ⅓ cup sugar with cinnamon. Roll puffs in cinnamon-sugar mixture. Makes 28 to 30 puffs.

How to Make Spicy Orange Puffs

Make a well in center of dry ingredients for orange juice and milk.

With tongs, roll cooked puffs in sugar-cinnamon mixture before serving.

Beignets (New Orleans Doughnuts)

So light and fluffy--like those from the French Quarter.

1 (¼-oz.) pkg. active dry yeast
  (1 tablespoon)
¾ cup warm water (110°F/45°C)
¼ cup sugar
½ teaspoon salt

1 egg
½ cup undiluted evaporated milk
3½ to 4 cups all-purpose flour
Vegetable oil for frying
Powdered sugar

■■■■■■■■ In a large bowl, dissolve yeast in water. Add sugar, salt, egg and evaporated milk. Gradually stir in 2 cups of flour. Beat until smooth. Add remaining flour, ⅓ cup at a time, beating to form a smooth firm dough. Cover and refrigerate overnight. On a lightly floured board, roll out dough about ⅜-inch thick, adding more flour if necessary. Cut in 3″ x 2″ rectangles or diamonds. Place several beignets into raised fryer basket. Lower into hot oil and fry 2 to 3 minutes or until golden brown. Turn for even browning. Drain and sprinkle with powdered sugar. Makes 22 to 26 beignets.

Raised Potato Doughnuts

Light, puffy and wonderful.

1 (¼-oz.) pkg. active dry yeast
  (1 tablespoon)
¼ cup warm water (110°F/45°C)
½ cup milk
2 tablespoons butter or margarine
¼ cup sugar

½ cup mashed potatoes
1 egg
¾ teaspoon salt
2¾ to 3¼ cups flour
Vegetable oil for frying
Sugar, if desired

■■■■■■■■ Combine dry yeast and warm water. In a small saucepan, heat milk, butter or margarine and sugar until butter or margarine begins to melt; cool to lukewarm. In a large bowl, combine mashed potatoes and egg. Stir in dissolved yeast, cooled milk mixture and salt. Gradually beat in flour to make soft dough. Turn out on a lightly floured board; knead until smooth. Place in a lightly buttered bowl; turn dough to butter top. Cover and let rise in a warm place 1 to 1½ hours or until doubled in bulk. Punch down and knead again. On a lightly floured board, roll out about ¼-inch thick. Cut with a floured doughnut cutter. Cover and let rise until doubled in bulk. Place several doughnuts into raised fryer basket. Lower into hot oil and fry 2 minutes or until brown. Drain and sprinkle with sugar, if desired. Makes 18 to 20 doughnuts.

Mincemeat Doughnuts

Perfect for a holiday brunch.

2 cups all-purpose flour
2 teaspoons baking powder
½ teaspoon salt
1 tablespoon butter or margarine,
  softened
¼ cup light corn syrup

1 teaspoon grated lemon peel
1 egg, beaten
1 cup mincemeat
Vegetable oil for frying
Sifted powdered sugar

▬▬▬▬▬▬ In a medium bowl, combine flour, baking powder and salt. In a large bowl, mix softened butter or margarine, corn syrup, grated lemon peel and egg. Add mincemeat. Stir in flour mixture. Chill 1 hour. On a lightly floured board, roll out dough about ½-inch thick. Carefully cut with a floured doughnut cutter; some of fruit pieces may be hard to cut. Place several doughnuts into raised fryer basket. Lower into hot oil and fry about 2 to 2½ minutes or until golden brown. Drain and sprinkle with powdered sugar. Makes 10 to 12 doughnuts.

Double-Chocolate Doughnuts

A dream-come-true for chocolate lovers!

1 egg
½ cup sugar
1 (1-oz.) square unsweetened chocolate
1 tablespoon butter or margarine
½ cup prepared mashed potatoes

1¾ cups all-purpose flour
3 teaspoons baking powder
½ teaspoon salt
⅓ cup milk
Vegetable oil for frying

Chocolate Frosting:
2 tablespoons butter or margarine
1 (1-oz.) square unsweetened chocolate
1 cup sifted powdered sugar

2 tablespoons boiling water
¼ teaspoon vanilla extract

▬▬▬▬▬▬ In a large bowl, beat egg until light. Beat in sugar. In a small saucepan, melt unsweetened chocolate and butter or margarine; add to egg mixture. Stir in potatoes. In a medium bowl, mix flour, baking powder and salt. Add milk alternately with flour mixture. Chill 1 hour. Prepare Chocolate Frosting. On a lightly floured board, roll out dough about ⅜-inch thick. Cut with a floured doughnut cutter. Place several doughnuts into raised fryer basket. Lower into hot oil and fry about 2 minutes or until crusty brown. Drain, cool and coat with Chocolate Frosting. Makes 12 to 14 doughnuts.

Chocolate Frosting:
In a small saucepan, melt butter or margarine and unsweetened chocolate. Beat in powdered sugar, boiling water and vanilla. Mix well.

Sour Cream Doughnuts

Firm-textured and flavorful.

1 egg
½ cup sugar
⅓ cup dairy sour cream
1½ cups all-purpose flour
½ teaspoon baking soda

1 teaspoon baking powder
⅛ teaspoon ground nutmeg
⅛ teaspoon salt
Vegetable oil for frying
Sugar or frosting, if desired

▬▬▬▬▬ In a large bowl, beat egg; gradually beat in sugar. Stir in sour cream. In a medium bowl, combine flour, baking soda, baking powder, nutmeg and salt. Fold into egg mixture; stir until smooth. Chill dough about 1 hour. On a lightly floured board, roll out dough about ⅜-inch thick. Cut with floured doughnut cutter. Place several doughnuts into raised fryer basket. Lower into hot oil and fry about 2 minutes or until golden brown. Drain and serve plain or sprinkle with sugar or frost, if desired. Makes 8 to 10 doughnuts.

Spicy Raised Doughnuts

So nice and spicy!

1 (¼-oz.) pkg. active dry yeast
   (1 tablespoon)
2½ cups all-purpose flour
1 teaspoon ground nutmeg
½ teaspoon ground cinnamon
1 cup milk

2 tablespoons sugar
1 teaspoon salt
2 tablespoons butter or margarine
1 egg
Vegetable oil for frying
Additional sugar or frosting, if desired

▬▬▬▬▬ In a medium bowl, combine yeast with 1 cup of flour, nutmeg and cinnamon. In a small saucepan, heat milk, 2 tablespoons sugar, salt and butter or margarine over low heat until very warm, 120°F to 130°F (49°C to 54°C). Add warm milk mixture to dry ingredients. Beat 2 minutes at medium speed, scraping bowl occasionally. Add ½ cup of flour and egg. Beat at high speed 2 minutes, scraping bowl occasionally. Stir in remaining 1 cup flour and mix well. Cover and let rise in a warm place until doubled in bulk. Turn out on a lightly floured board; shape in a soft ball. Roll out about ½-inch thick; let rise 20 minutes. Cut with a floured doughnut cutter. Place several doughnuts into raised fryer basket. Lower into hot oil and fry about 2 minutes or until golden brown. Drain. Serve plain or sprinkle with additional sugar or frost, if desired. Makes 12 doughnuts.

Apple Drop Doughnuts

No rolling out! Just drop into deep-fryer.

½ cup milk
¼ cup butter or margarine
¼ cup sugar
1 (¼-oz.) pkg. active dry yeast
  (1 tablespoon)
¼ cup warm water (110°F/45°C)
2 eggs
2¼ cups all-purpose flour

½ teaspoon salt
½ teaspoon grated lemon peel
1 cooking apple, cored, peeled, finely
  chopped
1 cup dark raisins or chopped dates
Vegetable oil for frying
½ cup sugar
1 teaspoon ground cinnamon

████████████ In a small saucepan, heat milk, butter or margarine and ¼ cup sugar until butter or margarine melts; set aside to cool. In a large bowl, dissolve yeast in warm water. Mix in cooled milk mixture and beat in eggs. In a medium bowl, combine flour, salt and grated lemon peel. Add ½ of flour mixture to liquid mixture, beating until well-blended. Beat in remaining flour. Stir in apple, raisins or dates. Cover and let rise in a warm place until doubled in bulk, about 1½ hours. Place fryer basket in lowered position. Spoon slightly heaping tablespoonfuls of dough into hot oil in deep-fryer. Fry about 2 minutes or until brown. Drain. Mix ½ cup sugar with cinnamon. Roll warm doughnuts in cinnamon-sugar mixture. Makes about 26 to 28 doughnuts.

Banana Doughnuts

If you like bananas, you'll love these doughnuts!

3½ to 4 cups all-purpose flour
1 (¼-oz.) pkg. active dry yeast
  (1 tablespoon)
¾ cup milk
⅓ cup shortening
¼ cup sugar
¾ teaspoon salt

1 egg
½ teaspoon grated lemon peel
½ cup mashed ripe banana (1 small
  banana)
Vegetable oil for frying
Powdered sugar

████████████ In a large bowl, stir together 1½ cups of flour and yeast. In a small saucepan, heat milk, shortening, sugar and salt just until warm, 120°F to 130°F (49°C to 54°C), stirring until shortening almost melts. Add to dry mixture with egg, grated lemon peel and mashed banana. Beat with an electric mixer on low speed 30 seconds, then at high speed 3 minutes. By hand, stir in 2 to 2½ cups of flour or enough to make a moderately soft dough. Turn out on a lightly floured board; knead until smooth and elastic, about 5 minutes. Place in a lightly buttered bowl. Turn dough to butter top. Cover and let rise until doubled in bulk, about 45 to 60 minutes. Punch down. Turn out on floured surface. Roll out dough about ½-inch thick. Cut with a floured doughnut cutter. Cover and let rise until nearly doubled in bulk, about 35 to 45 minutes. Place several doughnuts into raised fryer basket. Lower into hot oil and fry 2 to 3 minutes or until golden brown. Drain and cool. Sprinkle with powdered sugar. Makes 18 doughnuts.

Shortcut Raised Doughnuts

Hot-roll mix saves you time and effort.

1 (13¾-oz.) pkg. hot-roll mix
½ cup warm water (110°F/45°C)
2 egg yolks
½ cup dairy sour cream
½ teaspoon grated lemon peel

½ teaspoon ground nutmeg
3 tablespoons sugar
Vegetable oil for frying
Additional sugar, if desired

In a large bowl, dissolve package of yeast from hot-roll mix in warm water. Stir in egg yolks, sour cream, grated lemon peel, nutmeg and 3 tablespoons sugar. Add dry hot-roll mix; beat until well-blended. Cover and let rise in warm place 45 to 60 minutes or until doubled in bulk. On a lightly floured board, roll out dough ⅜-inch to ½-inch thick. Cut with a floured doughnut cutter. Cover and let rise about 30 minutes or until doubled in bulk. Place several doughnuts into raised fryer basket. Lower into hot oil and fry about 1½ to 2 minutes or until golden brown. Drain and coat with additional sugar, if desired. Makes 14 to 16 doughnuts.

For an overall coating of cinnamon-sugar, crumbs or grated cheese, place coating in a plastic bag. Drop in doughnut, fritter or fried vegetable; close bag and shake.

Many doughnuts are sprinkled with powdered sugar. For a fine sifted effect, place sugar in a strainer; hold above doughnuts and push through with a spoon.

Quickie Bismarcks

Children enjoy filling the holes with jelly.

1 (8-oz.) pkg. refrigerated biscuits
Vegetable oil for frying

Grape jelly
Sifted powdered sugar

▬▬▬▬▬ Separate biscuits. Place several biscuits into raised fryer basket. Lower into hot oil and fry about 2 minutes or until golden. Drain. While still warm, make a slit in center of doughnut side with a paring knife. Wiggle knife slightly to make a hole about ¾ way through each doughnut. Push ¼ teaspoon of jelly into each hole. Roll in powdered sugar. Makes 10 bismarcks.

Orange-Blossom Doughnuts

One of our favorites!

About 1¾ cups all-purpose flour
1 tablespoon sugar
½ teaspoon salt
1 (¼-oz.) pkg. active dry yeast
   (1 tablespoon)
½ cup milk

2 tablespoons water
1 tablespoon butter or margarine
1 egg
Vegetable oil for frying

Honey-Orange Sauce:
⅔ cup honey
⅓ cup orange juice

½ teaspoon grated orange peel

▬▬▬▬▬ Prepare Honey-Orange Sauce. In a medium bowl, thoroughly combine ¾ cup of flour, sugar, salt and yeast. In a small saucepan, heat milk, water and butter or margarine until butter or margarine begins to melt, about 120°F to 130°F (49°C to 54°C). Gradually add to dry ingredients. Beat 2 minutes with an electric mixer. Add egg and ½ cup of flour. Beat until smooth. Stir in enough additional flour to make a stiff batter. It will be consistency of a thick *batter*, not a dough. Cover; let rise in a warm place until doubled in bulk or about 1 hour. Stir down. Place fryer basket in lowered position. Drop batter by teaspoonful into hot oil and fry about 2 to 2½ minutes or until golden brown. Drain. While warm, dip into chilled Honey-Orange Sauce. Drain on wire racks. Makes 18 to 20 doughnuts.

Honey-Orange Sauce:
In a small saucepan, combine honey, orange juice and grated orange peel. Heat, stirring until well-blended. Chill several hours.

Dutch Doughnuts

Holland's traditional New Year's treat.

1 (¼-oz.) pkg. active dry yeast
   (1 tablespoon)
¼ cup warm water (110°F/45°C)
½ cup milk
¼ cup sugar
2¼ cups all-purpose flour
½ teaspoon salt
½ teaspoon grated lemon peel

2 eggs
1 large cooking apple, cored, peeled,
   chopped
½ cup currants
½ cup dark raisins
Vegetable oil for frying
½ cup sugar
1 teaspoon ground cinnamon

In a large bowl, combine yeast and water. Let stand several minutes, then add milk. In a medium bowl, mix ¼ cup sugar, flour, salt and grated lemon peel. Add ½ of flour mixture to liquid mixture, beating until well-blended. Add eggs, 1 at a time, beating after each. Beat in remaining flour mixture. Stir in apple, currants and raisins. Cover and let rise in a warm place until doubled in bulk, about 1½ hours. Place fryer basket in lowered position. Drop by tablespoonfuls into hot oil. Fry about 3 minutes or until brown. Drain. Mix ½ cup sugar with cinnamon. Dip doughnuts into cinnamon-sugar mixture. Makes 20 to 24 doughnuts.

Old-Fashioned Jelly Doughnuts

A favorite for kids of all ages.

¼ cup milk
2 tablespoons sugar
½ teaspoon salt
3 tablespoons butter
1 (¼-oz.) pkg. active dry yeast
   (1 tablespoon)
¼ cup warm water (110°F/45°C)

2 egg yolks
2 cups all-purpose flour
2 tablespoons jam or jelly
1 egg white
Vegetable oil for frying
Additional sugar

In a small saucepan, heat milk, 2 tablespoons sugar, salt and butter until butter begins to melt. Remove from heat and cool to lukewarm. In a large bowl, sprinkle yeast over warm water. Stir until dissolved. Add cooled milk mixture, egg yolks and 1 cup of flour. With an electric mixer, beat until smooth, about 2 minutes. With a wooden spoon or with hands, blend in remaining flour. Cover and let rise in a warm place until doubled in bulk, about 1½ hours. Punch down dough. Turn out on a lightly floured board; knead 10 minutes or until dough is smooth. Roll out ½ of dough about ¼-inch thick. Cut in 6 (3-inch) rounds. Place 1 teaspoon of jam or jelly in center of each round. Brush edges with egg white. Roll out remaining dough and cut out 6 more rounds. Place on top of jam- or jelly-filled rounds. Press edges to seal. Place on a lightly floured baking sheet. Cover with a towel and let rise until doubled in bulk, about 1 hour. Place several doughnuts into raised fryer basket. Lower into hot oil and fry 2½ to 3 minutes or until brown, turning once. Drain and sprinkle with additional sugar while warm. Makes 6 jelly doughnuts.

Glazed Yeast Doughnuts

Better than those you buy at the bakery!

1 (¼-oz.) pkg. active dry yeast
   (1 tablespoon)
¼ cup warm water (110°F/45°C)
¼ cup sugar
2 tablespoons butter or margarine

½ teaspoon salt
1 cup milk
3 to 3½ cups all-purpose flour
1 egg, well beaten
Vegetable oil for frying

Vanilla Glaze:
1 cup sifted powdered sugar
2 tablespoons milk

⅛ teaspoon vanilla extract

In a small bowl, dissolve yeast in warm water; set aside. In a medium saucepan, heat sugar, butter or margarine, salt and milk until butter or margarine melts. Cool to lukewarm. Pour into a large bowl and stir in ½ cup of flour. Beat until smooth. Stir in dissolved yeast. Add 1½ cups of flour; beat until smooth. Stir in egg. Stir in 1 to 1½ cups additional flour to make a soft dough. Turn out on a lightly floured board. Cover and let stand 5 minutes. Knead about 5 minutes. Place in a lightly buttered bowl. Turn dough to butter top. Cover and let rise in a warm place until doubled in bulk, about 1½ to 2 hours. Punch down. Turn out on lightly floured board. Roll out dough about ¼-inch thick. Cut with a floured cutter in doughnut shapes or 2-inch diamonds. Cover and let rise again until doubled in bulk, about 1 hour. Place several doughnuts into raised fryer basket. Lower into hot oil and fry 2 to 3 minutes or until golden brown. Drain. Prepare Vanilla Glaze. Dip top of warm doughnuts in Vanilla Glaze. Place doughnuts glaze-side-up on rack. Makes 25 to 30 doughnuts.

Vanilla Glaze:
In a small bowl, combine powdered sugar with milk and vanilla. Blend well.

After mixing ingredients, knead dough and place in a lightly buttered bowl. Cover and let rise in a warm place until the dough doubles its original size.

On a lightly floured board, roll out dough about ¼-inch thick. Cut with a doughnut cutter, then cover with wax paper or a clean cloth and let rise again.

How to Make Glazed Yeast Doughnuts

To prevent stretching dough out of shape, carefully slide pancake turner under each raised doughnut and gently place in raised fryer basket.

Fry doughnuts until golden brown. Drain on paper towels. While still warm, dip in glaze. Place on cooling rack.

Fish & Shellfish

There's no special trick to frying delicious fish and seafood. Fresh or frozen fillets of sole, cod and red snapper are really great. I like to use different kinds of coatings and a variety of sauces. These fillets make an ideal serving size. There is a lot of water around frozen fish fillets that are being thawed. Be very careful to dry frozen fish after it has completely thawed. Pour off excess water, then pat it dry with paper towels so there will be no water on the fish. Coatings are important on fish because they keep the center soft and moist, yet provide a crunchy outer layer.

Shrimp, scallops and oysters make a big hit when deep-fried. You may like to copy the popular seafood restaurants by serving your own Fisherman's Platter. You can combine fried fish fillets with shrimp and oysters or scallops. Cover all of them with the same coating or try a variety of your favorites.

Try shrimp fried in several different shapes, traditional shrimp, with or without tails, butterflied and fan-tailed. It isn't as complicated as it sounds. With a sharp knife and these directions, you can try several ways and maybe even discover a new shape for shrimp.

Don't forget to look through the chapter on sauces for interesting ways to top off your favorite fried-fish and seafood dishes.

Clockwise from top left: Crispy Beer Batter Fish, page 47; Butterfly Shrimp, page 45; Fried Scallops, page 47.

Fried Oysters

With large or small oysters, this recipe is sure to please.

1 (10-oz.) can oysters
⅓ cup all-purpose flour
½ teaspoon salt
⅛ teaspoon pepper
1 egg, slightly beaten
1 tablespoon water

⅔ cup fine cracker crumbs
Vegetable oil for frying
Lemon wedges
Tartar Sauce, page 148, or
Easy Seafood Sauce, page 148

━━━━━━━ Drain oysters. Pat dry with paper towels. Dip into a mixture of flour, salt and pepper in a shallow dish. Dip oysters into egg beaten with water in another shallow dish. Coat with cracker crumbs. Place fryer basket in lowered position. Fry in hot oil about 1½ to 2½ minutes or until golden brown. Drain and serve hot with lemon wedges and Tartar Sauce or Easy Seafood Sauce. Makes 4 servings.

Oyster-Potato Fries

A tasty dual flavor for oyster lovers.

2 tablespoons all-purpose flour
¼ teaspoon salt
¼ teaspoon seasoned salt
1 egg
1 teaspoon instant minced onion

2 tablespoons dairy sour cream
1 cup finely shredded uncooked
  potatoes
1 (10-oz.) can oysters, well drained
Vegetable oil for frying

━━━━━━━ In a small bowl, combine flour, salt and seasoned salt. In a medium bowl, beat egg. Stir in flour mixture, onion and sour cream. Pat potatoes dry and stir into egg-flour mixture. Pat oysters dry. Add 2 or 3 oysters at a time to potato mixture. Place fryer basket in lowered position. Using a spoon, drop several coated oysters into hot oil. Fry 3 to 4 minutes or until golden brown. Drain and serve hot. Makes 12 large oysters or 15 to 18 small oysters.

Almond-Crusted Scallops

Crunchy coating makes this deep-sea favorite irresistible.

1 lb. fresh or frozen scallops
¼ cup soft bread crumbs
¼ cup blanched almonds
½ cup all-purpose flour
½ teaspoon salt

¼ teaspoon pepper
1 egg, slightly beaten
2 tablespoons milk
Vegetable oil for frying

━━━━━━━━ Thaw scallops if frozen. Pat dry with paper towels. Combine bread crumbs and almonds in a food processor or blender. Process until mixture resembles fine crumbs. Set aside. In a shallow dish, dip scallops into flour mixed with salt and pepper, then dip scallops into egg mixed with milk in a small bowl. Dip scallops in bread crumb-almond mixture. Place several scallops into raised fryer basket. Lower into hot oil and fry 1 to 2 minutes or until golden. Drain and serve hot. Makes 4 to 5 servings.

Fried Teriyaki Scallops

Marinade gives oriental flavor to this New England favorite.

1 lb. fresh or frozen scallops
½ cup soy sauce
¼ cup white wine
2 tablespoons honey
½ teaspoon ground ginger

½ teaspoon garlic salt
½ cup all-purpose flour
½ cup milk
1 cup fine cracker crumbs
Vegetable oil for frying

━━━━━━━━ Thaw scallops if frozen. Pat dry with paper towels. In a medium bowl, combine soy sauce, wine, honey, ginger and garlic salt. Pour over scallops. Cover and refrigerate at least 1 hour. Drain thoroughly and pat dry. Place flour, milk and cracker crumbs separately in 3 small bowls. Dip marinated scallops into flour, then quickly into milk and coat with cracker crumbs. Place several scallops into raised fryer basket. Lower into hot oil and fry 1½ to 2 minutes or until brown and crisp. Drain and serve hot. Makes 4 to 5 servings.

Puffy Fried Shrimp

Very light and airy coating becomes crisp when fried.

1 lb. uncooked medium shrimp
1 egg, separated
1 tablespoon vegetable oil
½ cup flat beer
¾ cup cornstarch
½ teaspoon dry mustard
½ teaspoon salt
Vegetable oil for frying

Peel shrimp and remove vein. Pat dry with paper towels. In a medium bowl, beat egg yolk, 1 tablespoon oil and beer. In a small bowl, combine cornstarch, dry mustard and salt. Stir into egg yolk mixture. In a small bowl, beat egg white until stiff but not dry. Fold into egg yolk mixture. Dip shrimp into batter. Place several shrimp into raised fryer basket. Lower basket into hot oil and fry 2 to 3 minutes or until golden and crispy. Drain and serve hot. Makes 4 servings.

Sweet & Sour Fried Shrimp

A favorite that never fails to please.

1 lb. uncooked medium shrimp
½ cup all-purpose flour
¼ cup cornstarch
½ teaspoon baking powder
1 cup water
2 tablespoons vegetable oil
Vegetable oil for frying

Sweet & Sour Sauce:
1 (13-oz.) can pineapple tidbits
2 tablespoons dark-brown sugar
½ teaspoon salt
1 tablespoon cider vinegar
1 tablespoon soy sauce
1 tablespoon cornstarch
2 tablespoons water
1 small green bell pepper, cut in chunks

Prepare Sweet & Sour Sauce. Peel shrimp and remove vein. Pat dry with paper towels. In a small bowl, combine flour, cornstarch, baking powder, water and 2 tablespoons oil. Mix well. Dip shrimp into batter. Place several shrimp into raised fryer basket. Lower basket into hot oil and fry about 2 minutes or until golden. Drain and serve hot with Sweet & Sour Sauce. Makes 4 to 6 servings.

Sweet & Sour Sauce:
Drain pineapple, reserving syrup. In a saucepan, combine pineapple syrup, brown sugar, salt, vinegar and soy sauce. In a small bowl, dissolve cornstarch in water and add to syrup mixture. Cook over low heat, stirring constantly, until thickened and translucent. Stir in pineapple tidbits and bell pepper. Heat through. Keep warm.

Butterfly Shrimp

Palate-pleasing batter and an interesting shape lend a gourmet touch. (Photo on page 41.)

1 lb. uncooked large shrimp
1 cup buttermilk baking mix
2 eggs

½ cup cold water
½ teaspoon salt
Vegetable oil for frying

————— Peel shrimp and remove vein. Pat dry with paper towels. In a small bowl, combine baking mix, eggs, water and salt. Stir until smooth. Dip shrimp into batter. Place several shrimp into raised fryer basket. Lower basket into hot oil and fry 2 to 3 minutes or until golden brown. Serve hot. Makes 4 servings.

How To Make Butterfly Shrimp

To butterfly shrimp, peel shrimp, leaving tails on if desired. With a sharp knife, cut lengthwise along vein, but do not cut completely through.

Remove vein. Wash shrimp and pat dry. Open in butterfly fashion, being careful not to break apart.

Country-Fried Fish

A think crunchy coating that's easy to prepare.

1 lb. fresh or frozen fish fillets
⅓ cup undiluted evaporated milk
¾ cup fine cracker crumbs
1½ teaspoons salt

⅛ teaspoon pepper
Vegetable oil for frying
Tartar Sauce, page 148, if desired

█████████ Thaw fish if frozen. Pat dry with paper towels. Cut fillets crosswise in 2- to 3-inch pieces. In a shallow dish, dip fish into evaporated milk, then dip into cracker crumbs mixed with salt and pepper in another dish. Place several pieces into raised fryer basket. Lower into hot oil and fry 3 to 3½ minutes or until golden. Serve hot with Tartar Sauce, if desired. Makes 4 servings.

Southern-Fried Fish

A crunchy cornmeal coating.

1 lb. fresh or frozen fish fillets
1 egg, slightly beaten
2 tablespoons milk

½ cup cornmeal
½ teaspoon salt
Vegetable oil for frying

█████████ Thaw fish if frozen. Pat dry with paper towels. Combine egg and milk in a pie plate. Mix cornmeal and salt in another pie plate. Dip fish into egg mixture, then into cornmeal. Place several pieces into raised fryer basket. Lower into hot oil and fry 2 minutes on each side or until golden brown. Drain and serve hot. Makes 4 servings.

Crispy Fish Fillets

A thin crisp coating for your favorite fish fillets.

1 lb. fresh or frozen fish fillets
1 egg, slightly beaten
1 tablespoon water

¾ cup fine cracker crumbs
Vegetable oil for frying

█████████ Thaw fish if frozen. Pat dry with paper towels. Cut in serving-size pieces. In a shallow dish, dip fish into egg mixed with water, then into cracker crumbs in another dish. Place several pieces into raised fryer basket. Lower into hot oil and fry 3 minutes on each side or until brown and fish flakes easily with fork. Drain and serve hot. Makes 4 servings.

Fried Scallops

A quick deep-sea treat. (Photo on page 41.)

1 lb. fresh or frozen scallops
¼ cup all-purpose flour
½ teaspoon salt
1 egg, slightly beaten

1 tablespoon water
½ cup fine cracker or dry bread crumbs
Vegetable oil for frying

▬▬▬▬▬▬ Thaw scallops if frozen. Pat dry with paper towels. In a shallow dish, combine flour and salt. Roll scallops in flour mixture. In a small bowl, dip scallops into egg mixed with water, then coat with cracker or bread crumbs. Using fryer basket, fry in hot oil until golden, about 3 minutes. Drain and serve hot. Makes 4 servings.

Crispy Beer-Batter Fish

Beautiful golden batter that's crispy on the outside. (Photo on page 41.)

1 lb. fresh or frozen fish fillets
1¼ cups all-purpose flour
1 teaspoon baking powder
½ teaspoon salt

1 tablespoon vegetable oil
1 cup flat beer
Vegetable oil for frying

▬▬▬▬▬▬ Thaw fish if frozen. Pat dry with paper towels. In a medium bowl, combine 1 cup of flour, baking powder and salt. Make a well in center; pour in 1 tablespoon oil and beer. Stir until smooth. Cut fish fillets in crosswise strips about 2 to 3 inches wide. In a shallow dish, dip fish into ¼ cup of flour, then into batter. Using fryer basket, fry in hot oil about 2 minutes on each side or until golden. Drain and serve hot. Makes 4 servings.

Cracker-Coated Fish

Crispy coating with beautiful golden color.

1 lb. fresh or frozen fish fillets
½ cup all-purpose flour
½ teaspoon salt
⅛ teaspoon pepper
½ cup milk

¾ cup finely crushed cracker crumbs
  (about 20 saltine crackers)
Vegetable oil for frying
Lemon wedges, if desired
Tartar Sauce, page 148, if desired

▬▬▬▬▬▬ Thaw fish if frozen. Pat dry with paper towels. Cut in pieces about 2 inches wide. In a shallow dish, dip fillets into flour mixed with salt and pepper, then into milk in another dish, then in cracker crumbs. Using fryer basket, fry in hot oil 2 to 3 minutes or until golden. Drain and serve with lemon wedges and Tartar Sauce, if desired. Makes 4 servings.

Tempura Platter

A complete meal, encased in lacy tempura batter.

1 lb. uncooked shrimp or fish fillets
1 green bell pepper
2 medium zucchini
1 onion
1 sweet potato
2 eggs, beaten

¾ cup all-purpose flour
1 cup water
1 tablespoon cornstarch
½ teaspoon salt
½ teaspoon baking powder
Vegetable oil for frying

Peel shrimp, leaving tails on. Remove vein. Pat dry with paper towels. Cut fish crosswise in 2- to 3-inch pieces. Slice bell pepper and zucchini. Peel and slice onion and sweet potato. In a medium bowl, combine eggs, flour, water, cornstarch, salt and baking powder. Stir until well-blended, but do not beat. Dip fish and vegetables into batter immediately. Place fryer basket in lowered position. Fry a few pieces at a time in hot oil until golden. Drain and serve hot. Makes 4 servings.

Fan-Tail Shrimp

Here's an interesting way to prepare shrimp with a different shape.

1 lb. large uncooked shrimp
1 cup all-purpose flour
½ teaspoon salt
1 teaspoon sugar
1 egg, slightly beaten

1 tablespoon vegetable oil
1 cup cold water
Vegetable oil for frying
Easy Seafood Sauce, page 148,
   if desired

Peel shrimp, leaving tails on, if desired. Remove vein. Cut a slit through each shrimp starting about ½ inch from head and running to within ½ inch of tail. Pull tail through slit to make fan-tailed butterfly shape. Pat dry with paper towels. In a small bowl, combine flour, salt, sugar, egg, 1 tablespoon oil and cold water. Beat until almost smooth. Dip shrimp into batter and drain briefly. Using fryer basket, fry in hot oil about 2½ minutes or until golden. Drain and serve hot with Easy Seafood Sauce, if desired. Makes 4 servings.

Tempura Platter, above.

Fish Balls

A special idea for appetizer or entree.

1 lb. fresh or frozen fish fillets
2 cups water
½ teaspoon salt
2 slices white bread, crusts removed
⅓ cup milk
1 egg, slightly beaten
1 tablespoon ketchup

1 teaspoon minced instant dry onion
¼ teaspoon seasoned salt
½ cup fine dry bread crumbs
Vegetable oil for frying
Tartar Sauce, page 148, or Sweet & Sour
   Sauce, page 44, if desired

▬▬▬▬▬ Thaw fish if frozen. Pat dry with paper towels. In a large saucepan, heat water and salt to boiling. Add fish fillets. Simmer several minutes or until fish is tender. Drain fish and flake with a fork. Tear bread into small pieces, then soak in milk in a medium bowl. Add flaked fish, egg, ketchup, onion and seasoned salt. Shape in 1-inch balls. Roll in bread crumbs. Using fryer basket, fry in hot oil 1 to 1½ minutes. Drain and serve warm. Serve plain or with Tartar Sauce or Sweeet & Sour Sauce, if desired. Makes 22 to 24 balls.

Dixie Fish

For a less-concentrated cornmeal coating.

1 lb. fresh or frozen fish fillets
1 egg
1 tablespoon water
½ cup all-purpose flour
½ cup cornmeal

½ teaspoon salt
⅛ teaspoon pepper
Vegetable oil for frying
Lemon wedges
Tartar Sauce, page 148

▬▬▬▬▬ Thaw fish if frozen. Cut in pieces about 2 inches wide. Pat dry with paper towels. In a shallow dish, beat egg with water. Dip fish into egg mixture, then into flour mixed with cornmeal, salt and pepper in another dish. Using fryer basket, fry in hot oil 2 to 3 minutes or until golden brown and fish is done in center. Drain and serve hot with lemon wedges and Tartar Sauce, if desired. Makes 4 servings.

English-Style Fish

Make it fish 'n chips tonight!

1 lb. fresh or frozen fish fillets
¼ teaspoon salt
⅛ teaspoon pepper
About ½ cup all-purpose flour

1 egg, slightly beaten
⅓ cup milk
Vegetable oil for frying

■■■■■■■ Thaw fish if frozen. Cut in serving-size pieces. Pat dry with paper towels. Sprinkle fish with salt and pepper. Dip into ¼ cup of flour. In a shallow dish, mix egg, milk and remaining ⅓ cup flour. Dip floured fish into batter. Using fryer basket, fry in hot oil about 3 minutes or until done. Drain and serve hot. Makes 4 servings.

Variation

For fish 'n chips, serve with Traditional French Fries, page 80. Keep potatoes warm in 250°F (120°C) oven while frying fish or keep in covered deep-fryer with basket raised.

Walnut-Crusted Fish

Walnut coating gives an extra-special touch to fish.

1 lb. fresh or frozen fish fillets
½ cup soft bread crumbs
½ cup walnuts
½ cup all-purpose flour

½ teaspoon salt
1 egg
2 tablespoons milk
Vegetable oil for frying

■■■■■■■ Thaw fish if frozen. Process bread crumbs and walnuts in a food processor or blender until mixture resembles fine crumbs. Set aside. Cut fish in strips about 2 inches wide. Pat dry with paper towels. In a shallow dish, dip fish into flour mixed with salt, then into egg beaten with milk in another dish, then into crumb-nut mixture. Using fryer basket, fry in hot oil 1 to 2 minutes or until golden brown and crusty. Drain and serve hot. Makes 4 servings.

Poultry

Fried chicken is no longer a tradition limited to the Southern USA. When you try some of these chicken recipes, you'll want to start a similar tradition at your house, using your deep-fryer to produce golden, crunchy fried chicken.

While testing these recipes, I discovered several tips to pass along. Knowing that it takes a long time to deep-fry the thicker and larger chicken parts, I tried a variety of combinations of cooking processes. For example, when deep-fried, chicken wings came out OK, but larger pieces had a tendency to become dry and overdone on the outside before being done in the center. As a result, most recipes for chicken parts suggest that they be simmered for about twenty minutes before being fried. You can do this ahead of time, if you wish, then fry the chicken just before it is served.

The fry-bake method given in this section is convenient if you like to prepare the main dish ahead of time and heat it at the last minute. Fry-Baked Chicken, page 58, is ideal for entertaining because you can do the frying the night before; refrigerate the chicken, then put it in the oven to reheat and finish cooking while you visit with the guests. Frying gives the chicken a golden, crunchy texture that's sure to be a culinary delight.

If everyone in your family likes the same parts of chicken, you'll be ahead if you buy a package of one kind—and avoid arguments, too! Use identical pieces instead of a whole cut-up chicken and you will get lots of applause.

Batter-Fried Chicken, page 56.

Italian-Fried Chicken

Salad dressing gives chicken an Italian flavor.

1 (2½- to 3-lb.) frying chicken, cut up
¾ cup cornmeal
½ pkg. Italian salad dressing mix
   (about ½ oz.)

¼ cup whipping cream
Vegetable oil for frying

In a large saucepan, cover chicken with water. Cover and simmer about 20 minutes. Drain and pat dry with paper towels. In a shallow dish, combine cornmeal and dry salad mix. In a small bowl, dip chicken pieces into cream, then into cornmeal mixture. Place several pieces into raised fryer basket. Lower into hot oil and fry 2 to 3 minutes or until brown and crispy. Drain and serve hot. Makes 4 servings.

Paper-Wrapped Chicken

Have you ever fried with paper?

2 cups skinned boned uncooked
   chicken, cut in 1-inch squares
½ teaspoon salt
½ teaspoon sugar
1 tablespoon soy sauce

1 tablespoon white wine
5 green onions, cut in ½-inch pieces
Parchment paper, cut in 5- or 6-inch
   squares
Vegetable oil for frying

In a medium bowl, combine chicken, salt, sugar, soy sauce and wine. Mix well and refrigerate several hours. Place 2 squares of chicken and 1 piece of onion on each piece of parchment. Roll up and twist ends. Place several pieces into raised fryer basket. Lower into hot oil and fry about 2 minutes. Drain and serve hot. Carefully unwrap and remove parchment at table. Makes about 30 to 35 packets.

Note:
Parchment paper can be found in gourmet shops, hardware stores and the housewares section of department stores.

Sesame Chicken Nuggets with Ginger Sauce

Enjoy these for a quick Sunday night supper.

⅓ cup sesame seeds
¾ cup all-purpose flour
½ teaspoon salt
½ teaspoon pepper
½ teaspoon baking powder
¾ cup beer, room temperature

¼ cup minced fresh parsley
¼ teaspoon hot-pepper sauce
2 cloves garlic, minced
2 (½-lb.) skinned boned chicken
   breasts, cut in 1-inch pieces
Vegetable oil for frying

Ginger Sauce:
½ cup light corn syrup
2 tablespoons grated ginger root

2 tablespoons water
1 tablespoon lemon juice

Prepare Ginger Sauce. In a large skillet, toast sesame seeds over medium-high heat, stirring constantly, until lightly browned. In a medium bowl, combine sesame seeds, flour, salt, pepper and baking powder. Stir in beer, parsley, hot-pepper sauce and garlic until blended. Dip chicken pieces into batter. Place several pieces into raised fryer basket. Lower into hot oil and fry 2 to 3 minutes or until golden brown. Drain and serve hot with Ginger Sauce. Makes about 4 servings.

Ginger Sauce:

In a medium saucepan, combine corn syrup, ginger root, water and lemon juice. Bring to a boil, stirring occasionally, over medium heat. Reduce heat to low and simmer, uncovered, 5 minutes. Keep warm.

Sesame Chicken Nuggets with Ginger Sauce, above.

Batter-Fried Chicken

A traditional batter for deep-fried chicken. (Photo on page 53.)

1 (2½- to 3-lb.) frying chicken, cut up
1 egg, slightly beaten
⅔ cup milk
1 cup all-purpose flour

1½ teaspoons baking powder
½ teaspoon salt
Vegetable oil for frying

In a large saucepan, cover chicken with salted water. Cover and simmer about 20 minutes. Drain well and pat dry with paper towels. In a medium bowl, combine egg and milk; stir in flour, baking powder and salt. Beat until smooth. Dip chicken into batter. Drain on a rack over wax paper. Place several pieces into raised fryer basket. Lower into hot oil and fry 2½ to 3 minutes on each side or until brown and done inside. Drain and serve hot. Makes 4 servings.

Spicy Batter-Fried Chicken

Crispy and nicely seasoned with a spicy coating.

1 (2½- to 3-lb.) frying chicken, cut up
1 cup all-purpose flour
1 teaspoon seasoned salt
1 teaspoon paprika
1 teaspoon garlic salt

½ teaspoon poultry seasoning
1 egg
½ cup milk
Vegetable oil for frying

In a large saucepan, cover chicken with water. Cover and simmer about 20 minutes. Drain thoroughly and pat dry with paper towels. In a pie plate, combine flour, seasoned salt, paprika, garlic salt, poultry seasoning and pepper. In a small bowl, beat egg and milk. Dip chicken into flour mixture, then into egg mixture and again into flour mixture. Using fryer basket, fry several pieces at a time in hot oil 3 to 4 minutes or until crispy and golden brown. Drain and serve hot. Makes 4 servings.

Herb-Fried Chicken

Just a hint of herbs.

1 (2½- to 3-lb.) frying chicken, cut up
4 cups chicken bouillon
1 egg
¼ cup milk
½ cup all-purpose flour

½ teaspoon fines herbes
1 teaspoon salt
¼ teaspoon pepper
Vegetable oil for frying

■■■■■■■■ In a large saucepan, cover chicken with bouillon. Cover and simmer 20 minutes. Drain and pat dry with paper towels; reserve bouillon for making gravy or soup, if desired. In a small shallow dish, beat egg with milk. Dip chicken into egg, then into a mixture of flour, fines herbes, salt and pepper. Place several pieces into raised fryer basket. Lower into hot oil and fry 3 to 4 minutes or until golden brown. Drain and serve hot. Makes 4 servings.

Peanutty Fried Chicken

Peanut butter and chicken go great together!

1 (2½- to 3-lb.) frying chicken, cut up
1 egg, beaten
½ cup peanut butter
½ teaspoon salt
⅛ teaspoon pepper

⅔ cup milk
¼ cup all-purpose flour
½ cup fine dry bread crumbs
Vegetable oil for frying

In a large saucepan, cover chicken with water. Cover and simmer about 20 minutes. Drain and pat dry with paper towels. In a small bowl, blend egg, peanut butter, salt and pepper. Gradually stir in milk. In a shallow bowl, coat chicken with flour; shake off excess. Dip chicken into peanut-butter mixture. Drain on a rack over wax paper. Coat with bread crumbs. Place several pieces into raised fryer basket. Lower into hot oil and fry until golden brown, about 2 minutes. Drain and serve hot. Makes 4 servings.

Fry-Baked Chicken

Fry it now, and bake when you're ready to eat!

1 (2½ to 3-lb.) frying chicken, cut up
½ teaspoon salt
⅛ teaspoon pepper
1 egg, slightly beaten

½ cup milk
½ cup all-purpose flour
Vegetable oil for frying

███████████ Sprinkle chicken with salt and pepper. In a shallow dish, combine egg and milk. Dip chicken into egg mixture, then into flour. Using fryer basket, fry several pieces at a time in hot oil 2 to 3 minutes or until golden brown. Drain and place in a shallow baking dish. Bake 30 to 40 minutes in a 350°F (175°C) oven. Makes 4 servings.

Chicken Bits with Tropical Relish

Peppy fruit relish adds zip to the crunchy chicken.

1 lb. boneless chicken thighs or breasts
¼ cup all-purpose flour
¼ teaspoon salt
⅛ teaspoon pepper
1 egg, beaten slightly

1 tablespoon water
1¼ cups crushed corn chips
  (about 5 oz.)
Vegetable oil for frying

Tropical Relish:
1 small papaya, peeled, coarsely chopped
1 kiwi fruit, peeled, coarsely chopped
1 jalapeño pepper, minced
1 tablespoon lime juice

1 tablespoon chopped chives
1 teaspoon finely chopped fresh cilantro
¼ teaspoon salt

███████████ Prepare Tropical Relish. Remove skin from chicken; cut in 1½-inch squares. In a small bowl, combine flour, salt and pepper. In another small bowl, combine egg and water. Dip chicken into flour mixture, then into egg mixture and then roll in crushed corn chips. Using fryer basket, fry 6 to 8 pieces at a time in hot oil 1½ to 2 minutes or until golden brown. Drain on paper towels. Serve hot with Tropical Relish. Makes 4 servings.

Tropical Relish:
In a small bowl, combine all ingredients.

Busy-Day Fried Chicken

Here's a good time-saving batter.

1 (2½- to 3-lb.) frying chicken, cut up
1 cup pancake mix

¾ cup water

━━━━━━━━━ In a large saucepan, simmer chicken in salted water 20 minutes. Drain well and pat dry with paper towels. In a small bowl, combine pancake mix with ¾ cup water. Beat several minutes to blend. Dip chicken into batter. Drain well on a rack over wax paper. Place several pieces into raised fryer basket. Lower into hot oil and fry 2 to 3 minutes or until golden brown. Drain and serve hot. Makes 4 servings.

Crunchy Bran Chicken

You'll love this crunchy golden chicken.

1 (2½- to 3-lb.) frying chicken, cut up
1 egg, beaten
1 cup milk
½ cup whole-bran cereal
¼ cup vegetable oil

¾ cup all-purpose flour
1 teaspoon baking powder
½ teaspoon seasoned salt
½ teaspoon onion salt
Vegetable oil for frying

━━━━━━━━━ In a large saucepan, simmer chicken in lightly salted water 20 minutes. Drain and pat dry with paper towels. In a small bowl, combine egg, milk, cereal and ¼ cup oil; let stand 5 minutes. In a medium bowl, stir together flour, baking powder, seasoned salt and onion salt. Add egg mixture. Stir until blended. Dip chicken pieces into batter, turning to coat all sides. Drain on a rack over wax paper. Using fryer basket, fry several pieces at a time in hot oil about 2 minutes or until golden brown. Drain and serve hot. Makes 4 servings.

Chicken Kiev

The ultimate in elegance!

½ cup butter, softened
1 tablespoon finely chopped fresh
    parsley
1 teaspoon minced chives
½ teaspoon tarragon
1 small clove garlic, crushed
½ teaspoon salt

⅛ teaspoon pepper
3 whole chicken breasts, skinned,
    boned
⅓ cup all-purpose flour
1 egg, slightly beaten
½ cup fine dry bread crumbs
Vegetable oil for frying

▬▬▬▬▬▬ In a small bowl, mix butter with parsley, chives, tarragon, garlic, salt and pepper. Form into a 3-inch square. Freeze until firm. Cut chicken breasts in half. With a wooden mallet, pound chicken about ¼-inch thick, being careful not to break meat. Cut butter mixture in 6 pats. Place 1 pat in center of each piece of chicken. Bring sides and ends of chicken over butter mixture, making sure no butter mixture is showing. Fasten with wooden picks. In a pie plate, roll each in flour. In a small bowl, dip chicken into egg, then into bread crumbs. Refrigerate about 1 hour. Using fryer basket, fry several pieces of chicken at a time in hot oil until browned, about 6 minutes. Drain and serve hot. Makes 6 servings.

Bouillon-Fried Chicken

Give chicken extra flavor with bouillon coating.

1 (2½- to 3-lb.) frying chicken, cut up
½ cup all-purpose flour
½ teaspoon salt
1 cup buttermilk
¾ cup fine dry bread crumbs

1 teaspoon seasoned salt
¼ teaspoon seasoned pepper
¼ teaspoon celery salt
1 chicken bouillon cube, finely crushed
Vegetable oil for frying

▬▬▬▬▬▬ In a large saucepan, cover chicken with water. Bring to a boil, cover and simmer about 20 minutes. Drain and pat dry with paper towels. In 3 shallow dishes, dip chicken into flour mixed with salt, then into buttermilk and then into a mixture of bread crumbs, seasoned salt, seasoned pepper, celery salt and crushed bouillon. Using fryer basket, fry several pieces at a time in hot oil 3 to 4 minutes or until golden brown. Drain and serve hot. Makes 4 servings.

Mix softened butter with seasonings. Form in a three-inch square and freeze.

How To Make Chicken Kiev

While seasoned butter is frozen, cut in six equal pats—one for each piece of chicken.

Carefully fold sides and ends of chicken over butter mixture, making sure no butter is showing.

Main Dishes

A deep-fried entree is a savory answer to the eternal question of what to serve. The variety is practically unlimited, ranging from croquettes to sandwiches to spareribs.

Croquettes are impressive to serve, and also budget-stretchers. Next time you have leftover turkey, ham or chicken, consider grinding or chopping it and using it in one of these croquette recipes. Be aware that croquettes do take preparation time. Usually the sauce and meat should be refrigerated before being shaped. If the mixture is cool, it's easier to shape and can be coated more efficiently. Don't skimp on the coating for croquettes. If the recipe calls for a coating of flour, then egg, and then crumbs, follow each step carefully. Finally, chill the coated croquettes if suggested in the recipe. That second chilling process "sets" the coating and provides a shield around the meat and sauce. The result is a beautiful golden-brown crust with a moist, flavorful center. Although you may be used to croquettes in the familiar cone shape, small rectangles or log shapes are attractive to serve also.

Thick French Toast, page 73, is one of my favorite brunch or luncheon main dishes. It is so light and puffy when made with thick egg bread. Ordinarily, it is necessary to buy unsliced bread at a bakery, then slice it yourself. If it is not convenient for you to find this kind of unsliced bread, you can use regular bread that is available in any market.

Fried Cheese Sandwiches, page 72, are delicious. First, make a sandwich of mozzarella cheese, with or without thin slices of pastrami or pepperoni. This is coated with milk and crumbs to give a crunchy exterior, then dipped into an egg mixture and fried.

Perhaps you didn't realize that many sparerib dishes that are so popular in Chinese restaurants are fried. Simmer them first to make them more tender. Drain them thoroughly; fry until brown and crispy. Fried Glazed Spareribs, page 68, have a glaze with a snappy flavor. Sweet-Sour Ribs, page 64, are served with a more traditional oriental sweet & sour sauce.

Clockwise from top left: Mini-Potato Puffs, page 87; green beans; Milanese Cutlets, page 64; bell pepper salad.

Milanese Cutlets

A main dish worthy of a special occasion. (Photo on cover and on page 63.)

4 (3-oz.) lean boneless pork or veal cutlets or pork chops
2 eggs, beaten slightly
½ cup grated Parmesan cheese
¼ cup dry bread crumbs

2 tablespoons milk
⅛ teaspoon paprika
½ teaspoon seasoned salt
Vegetable oil for frying

▬▬▬▬▬ Trim all fat from edges of cutlets. With a meat mallet, pound cutlets to about ⅜-inch thickness. In a medium bowl, combine eggs, cheese, bread crumbs, milk, paprika and seasoned salt. Dip cutlets into coating. Place several cutlets into raised fryer basket. Lower into hot oil and fry about 3 minutes or until cutlets are no longer pink in center. Drain and serve hot. Makes 4 servings.

Sweet-Sour Ribs

Solve your menu problem with these succulent ribs.

2 lbs. spareribs
2 tablespoons cornstarch
2 tablespoons soy sauce

½ teaspoon salt
2 tablespoons honey
Vegetable oil for frying

Sweet & Sour Sauce:
1 tablespoon cornstarch
2 tablespoons brown sugar
2 tablespoons cider vinegar

1 tablespoon soy sauce
1 (8-oz.) can pineapple chunks,
undrained

▬▬▬▬▬ Cut ribs in 1- or 2-rib pieces. In a large saucepan, cover ribs with water. Bring to a boil and simmer 20 minutes. Meanwhile, prepare Sweet & Sour Sauce. Drain ribs thoroughly and pat dry with paper towels. In a shallow dish, combine cornstarch, soy sauce, salt and honey. Blend well. Coat drained ribs with honey mixture. Place several ribs into raised fryer basket. Lower into hot oil and fry about 1 minute or until brown and crispy. Drain. Spoon Sweet & Sour Sauce over fried ribs and serve warm. Makes 4 servings.

Sweet & Sour Sauce:
In a small saucepan, combine cornstarch and brown sugar. Stir in vinegar and soy sauce. Add pineapple chunks with juice. Cook, stirring constantly, until sauce is thick and translucent. Cover and keep warm.

Pizza Balls

Here's a meatball for all pizza fans.

1 egg
1 cup soft bread crumbs
½ cup milk
½ teaspoon garlic salt
⅛ teaspoon pepper
2 tablespoons instant minced onion
½ teaspoon oregano

1 lb. lean ground beef
1½ to 2 oz. Monterey Jack cheese,
  cut in ½-inch cubes
¼ cup all-purpose flour
Vegetable oil for frying
1 (8- to 10-oz.) can pizza sauce

━━━━━━━━━ In a medium bowl, beat egg. Stir in bread crumbs, milk, garlic salt, pepper, onion and oregano. Mix in beef. Shape 1 rounded tablespoon of meat mixture in a ball, placing a cheese cube in center. Coat with flour. Place several balls into raised fryer basket. Lower into hot oil and fry about 3 minutes or until brown. Drain. In a small saucepan, heat pizza sauce. Serve over hot fried meatballs. Makes 20 to 25 balls.

Turkey & Ham Croquettes

A great way to glamorize leftovers.

¼ cup butter or margarine
¾ cup all-purpose flour
½ cup chicken broth
½ cup milk
1 cup minced cooked turkey or chicken
½ cup boiled or baked ham, finely
  chopped

1 teaspoon minced fresh parsley
⅛ teaspoon nutmeg
½ teaspoon seasoned salt
1 egg, slightly beaten
¼ cup seasoned bread crumbs
Vegetable oil for frying

━━━━━━━━━ In a large saucepan, melt butter or margarine. Add ¼ cup of flour and cook over low heat, stirring several minutes. Stir in broth and milk. Simmer another 2 to 3 minutes. Remove from heat. Add turkey or chicken, ham, parsley, nutmeg and seasoned salt. Butter a 9″ x 5″ loaf dish. Spread mixture evenly in dish. Cover and chill about 2 hours or until fairly firm. Cut in rectangles about 2″ x 1.″ In a shallow dish, coat rectangles with ½ cup of flour. In a small bowl, dip rectangles into egg, then roll in bread crumbs. Place several croquettes into raised fryer basket. Lower into hot oil and fry about 1½ to 2 minutes or until golden brown. Drain and serve hot. Makes 16 croquettes.

Turkey-Carrot Croquettes

This is good plain or served with cream sauce.

2 cups finely chopped cooked turkey or
   chicken
2 eggs, slightly beaten
1 (10½-oz.) can cream-of-chicken soup,
   undiluted
1 tablespoon Worcestershire sauce

¼ cup finely chopped onion
1 medium carrot, peeled, grated
1 cup fine dry bread crumbs
½ cup fine cracker crumbs
Vegetable oil for frying

■■■■■■ In a medium bowl, combine turkey or chicken, eggs, soup, Worcestershire sauce, onion, carrot and bread crumbs. Mix well. Cover and chill several hours. Shape in small logs about 2″ x 1.″ Roll logs in cracker crumbs. Place several croquettes into raised fryer basket. Lower into hot oil and fry 2 to 2½ minutes or until golden brown. Drain and serve hot. Makes about 25 croquettes.

Spring Rolls

Or do you call them egg rolls?

½ lb. uncooked shrimp in shell
½ cup uncooked lean pork
2 tablespoons vegetable oil
½ cup chopped celery
½ cup fresh or canned bean sprouts
4 medium mushrooms, chopped
1 tablespoon soy sauce
1 tablespoon sherry wine

½ teaspoon salt
1 tablespoon cornstarch
2 tablespoons water
12 to 16 egg roll skins
Vegetable oil for frying
Mustard or Quick Chinese-Plum
   Sauce, page 147, if desired

■■■■■■ Peel and clean shrimp. Finely chop shrimp and pork. In a large skillet, heat 2 tablespoons oil. Add shrimp, pork and celery. Stir-fry several minutes, then add bean sprouts, mushrooms, soy sauce, wine and salt. Heat to boiling. Dissolve cornstarch in water. Add to meat mixture. Cook over low heat, stirring constantly, until thick and translucent. Place about 2 tablespoons of mixture diagonally across bottom of each egg roll skin. Fold bottom corner up over filling. Fold side corners in toward center. Roll up, brush water on edges and press to seal. Place several rolls into raised fryer basket. Lower into hot oil and fry 1½ to 2 minutes or until golden and crisp. Serve plain or with mustard or Quick Chinese-Plum Sauce, if desired. Cut into 1-inch slices for appetizers or leave whole for entree. Makes 12 to 16 rolls.

Note:
Egg roll skins or wrappers are available in oriental markets, gourmet shops and the frozen-food or deli sections of many supermarkets.

Salmon Balls

Mini-croquettes for a main dish.

1 medium potato, peeled
1 medium onion, peeled
1 (1-lb.) can salmon, drained, flaked
1½ tablespoons all-purpose flour
1 egg, slightly beaten

½ teaspoon salt
⅛ teaspoon pepper
½ cup fine dry bread crumbs
Vegetable oil for frying
1 (10-oz.) pkg. frozen creamed peas

▬▬▬▬▬ In a medium bowl, coarsely grate potato and onion. Add salmon, flour, egg, salt and pepper. Mix well. Shape in 20 to 24 balls about 1 inch in diameter. In a shallow dish, roll balls in bread crumbs. Refrigerate at least 1 hour. Using fryer basket, fry in hot oil about 2 minutes or until brown. Drain well. Prepare creamed peas according to package directions. Serve over hot Salmon Balls. Makes 4 to 5 servings.

Chicken-Almond Croquettes

Next time try ham instead of chicken.

3 tablespoons butter or margine
3 tablespoons all-purpose flour
1 cup milk
¼ teaspoon salt
¼ teaspoon garlic salt
½ teaspoon chili powder
½ cup chopped almonds

1½ cups finely ground cooked chicken
  or turkey
1 tablespoon lemon juice
¾ cup fine dry bread crumbs
1 egg
1 tablespoon water
Vegetable oil for frying

▬▬▬▬▬ In a medium saucepan, melt butter or margarine over moderate heat. Stir in flour. Slowly stir in milk. Add salt, garlic salt and chili powder. Cook, stirring until thick. Remove from heat. Add almonds, chicken or turkey and lemon juice. Spread mixture on a platter to cool. Shape in 12 logs. Roll in bread crumbs. Let stand about 5 minutes. In a small bowl, beat egg and water. Dip each log into egg mixture. Roll again in bread crumbs. Refrigerate croquettes 30 minutes. Using fryer basket, fry in hot oil 2 to 2½ minutes. Turn and fry another 2 minutes. Drain and serve hot. Makes 12 croquettes.

Rhineland Kabobs

Try these kabobs for an extra special dinner.

8 to 10 oz. boneless pork cutlet or beef
    tenderloin
4 oz. calf liver, if desired, cut in 1-inch
    pieces
4 oz. ham, cut in 1-inch pieces
3 large green onions, trimmed, cut in
    1-inch pieces
1 small red or green bell pepper, cut in
    1-inch pieces

1 onion, if desired, cut in wedges
4 to 6 mushrooms
Vegetable oil for frying
Salt and pepper
⅓ cup dairy sour cream
2 teaspoons chopped chives

Honey Mustard Sauce:

2 tablespoons Dijon-style mustard
4 teaspoons honey

1 teaspoon prepared horseradish
½ cup dairy sour cream

■■■■■■■■■ Soak 4 to 6 (8-inch) bamboo skewers in water before piercing meat and vegetables. Prepare Honey Mustard Sauce. Trim fat off edges of pork or beef; cut in 1-inch pieces. Thread pork or beef onto bamboo skewers alternately with liver, if desired, ham, green onions, bell pepper, onion, if desired, and mushrooms. Using fryer basket, fry 2 at a time in hot oil 2 to 2½ minutes or until meat is no longer pink. Drain and sprinkle with salt and pepper. Serve with Honey Mustard Sauce or top with sour cream and chives. Makes 4 to 6 kabobs.

Honey Mustard Sauce:
In a small bowl, combine all sauce ingredients.

Fried Glazed Spareribs

Spareribs with a new look and great taste.

2 lbs. spareribs
1 tablespoon soy sauce
1 egg, slightly beaten

¼ cup all-purpose flour
Vegetable oil for frying

Soy-Onion Glaze:

½ cup sugar
½ cup wine vinegar

¼ cup soy sauce
2 tablespoons sliced green onions

■■■■■■■■■ Cut spareribs in 1- or 2-inch pieces. In a large saucepan, cover ribs with water. Bring to a boil, then simmer 20 minutes. Meanwhile, prepare Soy-Onion Glaze. Drain thoroughly and pat dry with paper towels. In a shallow dish, combine soy sauce, egg and flour. Brush spareribs with egg mixture. Place several ribs into raised fryer basket. Lower into hot oil and fry 2 to 3 minutes or until brown and crispy. Drain well. Brush hot fried spareribs with Soy-Onion Glaze. Makes 4 servings.

Soy-Onion Glaze:
In a small saucepan, cook sugar, wine vinegar, soy sauce and green onion over medium heat, stirring constantly, until mixture is syrupy. Cover and keep warm.

Rhineland Kabobs, above.

Egg Croquettes

Bite into these crusty croquettes with a soft egg mixture inside.

2 tablespoons butter or margarine
½ cup plus 2 tablespoons all-purpose
   flour
½ cup milk
4 hard-cooked eggs, finely chopped
1 tablespoon grated onion
2 tablespoons finely chopped fresh
   parsley

½ teaspoon dry mustard
½ teaspoon celery salt
⅛ teaspoon pepper
1 egg, slightly beaten
1½ cups soft bread crumbs
Vegetable oil for frying

In a heavy saucepan, melt butter or margarine. Stir in 2 tablespoons of flour. Pour in milk, stirring constantly. Bring to a boil. Stir and simmer several minutes. Remove from heat. Add hard-cooked eggs, onion, parsley, dry mustard, celery salt and pepper. Refrigerate mixture several hours or until thoroughly chilled. Divide mixture in 6 equal parts. Shape each in a cylinder about 3 inches long and 1 inch in diameter. In a shallow dish, dip cylinders in ½ cup of flour. In a small bowl, dip cylinders in egg, then roll in bread crumbs. Refrigerate another 20 to 30 minutes. Using fryer basket, fry in hot oil until golden. Drain and serve hot. Makes 6 croquettes.

Beef & Potato Mini-Meatballs

Meat 'n potatoes together make delicious mini-meatballs.

1 lb. lean ground beef
1 (12-oz.) pkg. frozen hash-brown potatoes, thawed
½ cup finely chopped onion
1 egg

1 teaspoon curry powder
½ teaspoon salt
¼ teaspoon pepper
Vegetable oil for frying
Sweet-Sour Sauce, page 44, if desired

In a medium bowl, mix together ground beef, potatoes, onion, egg, curry, salt and pepper. Form in 1-inch balls. Using fryer basket, fry in hot oil about 4 minutes or until done inside. Drain and serve hot. Serve plain or with Sweet-Sour Sauce, if desired. Makes 50 mini-meatballs.

Stir together sauce, cooked eggs and seasonings, then refrigerate several hours.

How To Make Egg Croquettes

Divide chilled mixture into six equal parts. Shape each part into a cylinder or "log."

Roll chilled cylinders in flour, then in egg and then in bread crumbs. Chill again before frying.

Ham & Scrambled Egg Croquettes

What a novel idea for brunch!

¼ cup butter or margarine
½ cup plus 2 tablespoons all-purpose
   flour
½ cup chicken broth
1½ cups finely chopped cooked ham

4 eggs, slightly beaten
1 tablespoon minced fresh parsley
¼ teaspoon salt
Vegetable oil for frying

━━━━━━━ In a small saucepan, melt 2 tablespoons of butter or margarine. Add 2 tablespoons of flour and cook over low heat, stirring several minutes. Stir in broth and simmer 2 to 3 minutes. In a large skillet, heat ham in 2 tablespoons of butter or margarine. Add eggs, parsley and salt. Scramble eggs until they form soft curds. Stir egg mixture into thickened chicken broth. Butter a 9″ x 5″ loaf dish and spread mixture evenly in dish. Cover and chill about 2 hours or until firm. Cut in 2″ x 1″ rectangles. Roll rectangles in ½ cup flour. Carefully drop into hot oil and fry 1½ to 2 minutes or until golden brown. Drain and serve hot. Makes 18 to 20 mini-croquettes.

Fried Cheese Sandwiches

This hearty Italian sandwich makes a meal!

16 slices Italian or French bread
½ lb. mozzarella cheese
½ cup plus 2 tablespoons milk
1 cup fine dry seasoned bread crumbs

4 eggs
Vegetable oil for frying
Marinated artichoke hearts or
   tomatoes, if desired

━━━━━━━ With a 3-inch cutter, cut slices of bread into rounds. Slice cheese ¼-inch thick. Make sandwiches of bread rounds and cheese. In a pie plate, briefly dip both sides of each sandwich in ½ cup of milk. Gently press edges together, then dip both sides in bread crumbs. To seal more securely, roll edges of sandwiches around slowly through bread crumbs. In a shallow dish, dip sandwiches into eggs mixed with 2 tablespoons of milk. Using fryer basket, fry in hot oil about 2 minutes or until brown on each side. Drain and serve hot with marinated artichoke hearts or tomatoes, if desired. Makes 8 sandwiches.

Variation:
Add several thin slices of cooked pastrami or pepperoni to cheese in each sandwich.

Scotch Eggs

Cut in wedges for appetizers or serve halves on a luncheon plate or tuck a whole Scotch Egg in a lunch box or picnic basket.

6 eggs
1 lb. pork sausage
¼ cup soft bread crumbs
2 tablespoons finely chopped fresh
   parsley

¼ cup finely chopped onion
½ teaspoon dried tarragon
⅓ cup all-purpose flour
Vegetable oil for frying

━━━━━━━━━ In a small saucepan, boil eggs about 10 minutes or until hard-cooked. Peel, pat dry and set aside. In a medium bowl, mix sausage with bread crumbs, parsley, onion and tarragon. Completely cover each egg with sausage mixture. Roll in flour. Place several eggs into raised fryer basket. Lower into hot oil and fry about 4 to 5 minutes or until brown on all sides and sausage is done. Sausage may crack occasionally while frying. Serve warm or cool. Makes 6 coated eggs.

French Toast

A classic favorite for breakfast, lunch or Sunday brunch.

2 eggs
⅓ cup milk
¼ teaspoon salt
4 (1-inch-thick) slices bread

Vegetable oil for frying
Maple syrup, honey or fruit-flavored
   syrup

━━━━━━━━━ In a shallow dish, beat eggs with milk and salt. Trim crusts from bread. Dip into egg mixture. Let stand a few seconds. Turn bread and repeat on other side. Using a fork, place bread into raised basket. Carefully lower bread into hot oil. Fry about 2 minutes or until golden brown. Drain and serve hot with maple syrup, honey or fruit-flavored syrup. Makes 4 slices.

Corn Dogs

Special summer fun served on skewers.

1 cup all-purpose flour
⅔ cups cornmeal
2 tablespoons sugar
1½ teaspoons baking powder
½ teaspoon salt
2 tablespoons shortening

1 egg, beaten
¾ cup milk
10 frankfurters
Vegetable oil for frying
Mustard and relish, if desired

In a medium bowl, mix flour, cornmeal, sugar, baking powder and salt. With a pastry blender or fork, cut in shortening until mixture resembles fine crumbs. In a small bowl, combine egg and milk. Add to dry mixture; mix well. Pat frankfurters dry with paper towels. Dip frankfurters into batter, being careful to coat all sides. Place several corn dogs into raised fryer basket. Lower into hot oil and fry until golden, about 1 minute on each side. Insert a wooden skewer in end of each, if desired. Serve hot with mustard and relish, if desired. Makes 10 corn dogs.

How to Make Corn Dogs

With a pastry blender or fork, cut shortening into flour mixture, then add egg and milk.

Dip frankfurters into batter with tongs; let excess batter drip off before frying.

Crispy Corn Dogs

Wooden skewers make these neater to eat!

10 frankfurters	3 tablespoons shortening
1½ teaspoons baking powder	1 egg, beaten
½ teaspoon salt	¾ cup milk
2 tablespoons yellow cornmeal	Vegetable oil for frying

━━━━━━━━━ Pat frankfurters dry with paper towels. In a medium bowl, combine flour, baking powder, salt and cornmeal. Cut in shortening thoroughly. Stir in egg and milk. Dip frankfurters into batter, allowing excess batter to drip into bowl. Place several corn dogs into raised fryer basket. Lower into hot oil and fry until golden brown, about 2 minutes. Insert a wooden skewer in end of each corn dog, if desired. Makes 10 crispy corn dogs.

Beefy Hot Dogs

Hamburger and hot dogs--prepared as a pair!

1 lb. lean ground beef	½ teaspoon salt
¾ cup soft bread crumbs	Dash pepper
¼ cup milk	6 frankfurters
2 tablespoons finely chopped onion	Vegetable oil for frying
1 egg, slightly beaten	6 hot dog buns

Ketchup Sauce:

1 cup ketchup	¼ cup molasses
¼ cup butter or margarine	2 tablespoons vinegar

━━━━━━━━━ Prepare Ketchup Sauce. In a large bowl, combine ground beef, bread crumbs, milk, onion, egg, salt and pepper. Mix lightly and divide in 6 portions. Shape beef mixture around frankfurters to cover completely. Cover and chill at least 1 hour. Place several frankfurters into raised fryer basket. Lower into hot oil and fry 2 minutes. Turn and fry another 2 minutes. Drop in warm Ketchup Sauce to coat. Serve on toasted buns. Makes 6 beefy hot dogs.

Ketchup Sauce:

In a small saucepan, combine ketchup, butter or margarine, molasses and vinegar. Simmer about 5 minutes. Cover and keep warm.

Potatoes

In the USA there is perhaps nothing more synonymous with deep-frying than French-fried potatoes. It is rare to see a hot dog or hamburger ordered in a fast-food establishment without French fries. Your deep-fryer makes excellent French fries—use it often to satisfy that French-fry craving. Potatoes prepared in a variety of ways are excellent when deep-fried, so don't miss out on the other distinctive tastes—try all the recipes in this section.

Let's talk first about "fries" and "chips." It is almost universally accepted that a really good French fry must first be soaked in water to remove starch, and be fried *twice*. If you are in a hurry, you can get by with frying them only once with satisfactory results. However, the second frying gives you superior quality. The results are more crisp and better tasting French fries with less shriveling.

For potato chips, the real secret is a very thin potato slice. You can do this with a very sharp knife, but I prefer to use a vegetable peeler.

The frying times given in the following recipes should be about right for the thickness of potatoes specified. However, frying time will vary with the thickness of the piece, moisture content and the quantity in the deep-fryer. Consequently you may have to experiment a bit at first. You'll quickly find correct timing for your particular cut of fries or chips. Just remember that the degree of doneness is in direct relation to the degree of bubbling. For instance; chips stop bubbling when done and fries bubble lazily when done.

In frying uncoated potatoes, it is difficult to remove all moisture by patting them with paper towels. Consequently, very active bubbling and some splattering will occur when the potatoes are lowered into the hot oil. If your deep-fryer came with a basket, use it. Keep your fryer lid locked. Raise and lower the basket from the outside as required. If you don't have a fryer basket, use a slotted spoon.

Traditional French Fries, page 80.

Natural French Fries

Unpeeled potatoes give more natural flavor to these French fries.

3 medium potatoes
Vegetable oil for frying

Seasoned salt to taste
Grated Parmesan cheese to taste

■■■■■■■ Wash potatoes thoroughly. Pat dry. Cut each in 8 wedges. In a medium bowl, soak wedges in cold water 30 minutes, changing water once. Drain and pat dry with paper towels. Place potatoes into raised fryer basket. Lower slowly into hot oil and fry 5 to 6 minutes. Raise basket and drain. Just before serving, fry again in hot oil 4 to 5 minutes or until brown and done inside. Drain. Sprinkle with seasoned salt and grated Parmesan cheese to taste and serve hot. Makes 4 servings.

Frozen Shredded Potato Rolls

Two minutes from freezer to table!

1 lb. frozen shredded potato rolls,
   such as Ore-Ida® Tater Tots®
Vegetable oil for frying

Salt to taste
Grated American or Parmesan cheese,
   if desired

■■■■■■■ Place several potato rolls into raised fryer basket. Lower into hot oil and fry 2 to 3 minutes or until golden brown. Drain and sprinkle with salt to taste. Serve hot. Sprinkle with grated American or Parmesan cheese, if desired. Makes 5 to 6 servings.

Food-Processor French Fries

These soft-centered potato slices complement any entree.

3 medium potatoes
Water

Vegetable oil for frying
Salt to taste

■■■■■■■ Peel potatoes and shape to fit processor's feed tube; feed through slicer. In a medium bowl, soak slices in cold water about 30 minutes, changing water once. Drain and pat dry with paper towels. Place several potato slices into raised fryer basket. Lower slowly into hot oil and fry 4 to 5 minutes or until golden brown. Raise basket and drain. Sprinkle with salt and serve hot. Makes 4 servings.

Favorite Potato Chips

A super potato chip! The extra effort pays big dividends in taste and crispness.

2 medium potatoes
Vegetable oil for frying

Salt to taste

Peel potatoes. Cut in very thin slices, less than 1/16-inch thick. In a medium bowl, soak in cold water 30 minutes, changing water once. Drain and pat dry with paper towels. Arrange slices in a single layer on a wire rack in a broiler pan. Place in a 250°F (120°C) oven 15 to 20 minutes. Place several slices into raised fryer basket. Lower into hot oil and fry 2 to 2½ minutes or until crisp and golden. Drain and sprinkle with salt to taste while hot. Makes 60 to 80 chips, depending on size of potatoes and thickness of slices.

Note:
A vegetable peeler is ideal for slicing potatoes for chips. The slicer on a hand grater may also be used.

Pre-Salted Potato Chips

Salting before frying makes a crisper chip.

2 medium potatoes
Salt

Vegetable oil for frying

Peel potatoes. Cut in very thin slices, less than 1/16-inch thick. In a medium bowl, soak in cold water 20 to 30 minutes, changing water once. Drain and pat dry with paper towels. Arrange a single layer of potato slices on bottom of a pie plate. Sprinkle lightly with salt. Repeat layering and salting potato slices until all are arranged in pie plate. Cover with plastic wrap and let stand about 1 hour. Drain and pat dry with paper towels. Place several slices into raised fryer basket. Lower into hot oil and fry 2 to 2½ minutes or until golden brown and crisp. Drain and serve hot. Makes 60 to 80 chips, depending on size of potatoes and thickness of slices.

Traditional French Fries

Good basic French fries! (Photo on pages 77 & 83.)

3 medium potatoes
Vegetable oil for frying
Salt to taste

━━━━━━━━━━ Peel potatoes. Cut in ¼- to ½-inch thick strips. In a medium bowl, soak potato strips in cold water 30 minutes, changing water once. Drain and pat dry with paper towels. Place potatoes into raised fryer basket. Lower slowly into hot oil and fry 5 to 6 minutes. Raise basket and drain. Just before serving, fry again in hot oil 4 to 5 minutes or until golden brown and done inside. Drain. Sprinkle with salt to taste and serve hot. Makes 4 servings.

Hash-Brown Haystacks

They resemble hash browns--but taste even better.

1 small onion
3 large potatoes
2 eggs, separated

½ teaspoon salt
Vegetable oil for frying
Applesauce or sour cream, if desired

━━━━━━━━━━ Peel, grate and drain onion and potatoes. In a small bowl, beat egg whites until stiff and dry. In a medium bowl, combine well-drained onions and potatoes, slightly beaten egg yolks and salt. Fold in beaten egg whites. Place fryer basket in lowered position. Immediately drop by tablespoonfuls into hot oil. Fry until golden brown, 2 to 3 minutes. Drain. Serve plain or topped with applesauce or sour cream, if desired. Makes about 4 servings.

Delta French Fries

A cheesy twist to the ever-popular French fries.

2 large potatoes
1 egg
1 tablespoon water
¾ cup (about 16) finely crushed cheese
   crackers

Vegetable oil for frying
Salt to taste

▬▬▬▬▬▬▬ Peel potatoes and cut in sticks like French fries. In a medium bowl, soak sticks in cold water 30 minutes; change water once. In a small bowl, beat egg slightly with water. Drain potatoes and pat dry with paper towels. Dip potatoes into egg mixture, then into cracker crumbs. Place fryer basket in lowered position. Fry potatoes in hot oil about 4 to 5 minutes or until brown. Raise basket and drain several minutes. Sprinkle with salt to taste and serve hot. Makes 4 servings.

Pre-Baked French Fries

Oven-baked potatoes provide a more flavorful French fry.

2 medium potatoes
Vegetable oil for frying

Salt to taste

▬▬▬▬▬▬▬ Peel potatoes. Cut in ¼- to ½-inch thick strips. In a medium bowl, soak in cold water 30 minutes, changing water once. Drain and pat dry with paper towels. Arrange potato strips in a single layer on a wire rack in a broiler pan. Bake in a 250°F (120°C) oven 20 minutes. Place several strips into raised fryer basket. Lower into hot oil and pre-fry 1½ to 2 minutes. Drain and let stand to cool at least 10 minutes. Just before serving, fry again in hot oil 5 to 6 minutes or until golden and done inside. Drain and sprinkle with salt. Serve hot. Makes 3 to 4 servings.

Potato Fingers

Similar to mini-croquettes.

1 lb. potatoes (4 medium), peeled,
   quartered
1 tablespoon milk
2 tablespoons butter or margarine
1 tablespoon sauterne wine
1 egg yolk, beaten slightly

½ teaspoon salt
1 egg white
1 tablespoon water
½ cup dry bread crumbs
Vegetable oil for frying

In a medium saucepan, cook potatoes in boiling water 20 minutes or until tender; drain. In a medium bowl, mash potatoes. Add milk, butter, wine, egg yolk and salt. Beat until smooth. Cover and chill. Divide potato mixture in quarters. On a lightly floured board, roll each quarter into a rope about 15″ x ¾.″ Cut each rope in 6 (2½-inch) pieces. In a small bowl, combine egg white and water. Beat slightly. Dip potato pieces into egg white mixture, then into bread crumbs. Chill again. Place several fingers at a time into raised fryer basket. Lower into hot oil and fry about 1 minute or until golden. Serve hot. Makes 24.

Traditional Potato Chips

There is nothing quite so good as freshly fried potato chips.

2 medium potatoes
Vegetable oil for frying

Salt to taste

Peel potatoes. Cut in very thin slices, less than ¹⁄₁₆-inch thick. Soak in cold water 20 to 30 minutes, changing water once. Drain and pat dry with paper towels. Place about a dozen slices into raised fryer basket. Lower into hot oil and fry 2 to 2½ minutes or until golden brown and crisp. Drain and sprinkle with salt to taste. Makes 60 to 80 chips, depending on size of potatoes and thickness of slices.

Note:
A vegetable peeler is ideal for slicing potatoes for chips. The slicer on a hand grater may also be used.

Traditional Potato Chips, above; Potato Fingers, above; Traditional French Fries, page 80.

Potato Balls

Superb taste compensates for the time you spend.

4 medium potatoes, peeled, cooked,
  mashed
2 tablespoons butter or margarine
½ cup shredded Cheddar cheese (2 oz.)
½ teaspoon salt
2 tablespoons half-and-half cream
2 egg yolks, slightly beaten

½ teaspoon baking powder
½ cup all-purpose flour
1 whole egg
2 tablespoons water
¾ cup fine dry bread crumbs
Vegetable oil for frying

In a medium bowl, combine mashed potatoes, butter or margarine, cheese, salt, half-and-half cream, egg yolks and baking powder. Shape in 1½-inch balls. In shallow dishes, roll balls in flour, then dip into egg slightly beaten with water and then dip balls into bread crumbs. Refrigerate 1 hour. Place several balls into raised fryer basket. Lower into hot oil and fry until brown, about 1 to 1½ minutes. Drain and serve hot. Makes 22 to 25 balls.

How To Make Potato Balls

Bake potatoes until tender, peel and mash. Add cheese, egg yolks and other ingredients to form balls.

Before frying, roll potato balls in flour, whole-egg mixture and bread crumbs, then refrigerate.

Potato Clouds

Rain or shine, you can count on these to please!

½ cup all-purpose flour
1 teaspoon baking powder
¼ teaspoon salt
1 cup cooked mashed potatoes

1 egg, slightly beaten
1 teaspoon minced chives
1 teaspoon fresh parsley
Vegetable oil for frying

▬▬▬▬▬ In a medium bowl, combine flour, baking powder, salt, mashed potatoes, egg, chives and parsley. Place fryer basket in lowered position. Drop batter by teaspoonfuls into hot oil. Fry until golden, about 2 to 2½ minutes. Drain and serve hot. Makes 18 potato clouds.

Mock Pommes Soufflés

Crisp outside and hollow inside like the famous French potato puff.

3 medium potatoes, peeled, cooked,
    mashed
¼ teaspoon onion salt
⅛ teaspoon pepper

¼ teaspoon seasoned salt
1½ cups all-purpose flour
¼ cup sour cream
Vegetable oil for frying

▬▬▬▬▬ In a large bowl, mix potatoes, onion salt, pepper, seasoned salt and 1 cup of flour. Stir in sour cream. Mixture should be a thick dough. Knead several times on a lightly floured board. Form in 1-inch balls. Flatten balls with a rolling pin to make a thick oval. In a pie plate, dip balls into ½ cup of flour. Place several soufflés in raised fryer basket. Lower into hot oil and fry about 2 minutes or until golden and puffy. Drain and serve hot. Makes 30 to 35 puffs.

Matchstick Potatoes

Mini-version of standard French fries.

2 medium potatoes
Vegetable oil for frying

Salt to taste

━━━━━━━━━━ Peel potatoes. Cut in slices about ⅛-inch thick. Cut each slice in very thin sticks, about size of a kitchen match. In a medium bowl, soak in cold water a few minutes. Drain thoroughly and pat dry with paper towels. Place several matchsticks into raised fryer basket. Lower into hot oil and fry 1½ to 2 minutes or until golden brown. Drain and sprinkle with salt to taste. Serve hot. Makes 2 to 3 servings.

Potato Nests

Get bird's nest baskets from your gourmet shop for this specialty.

2 medium potatoes, peeled
Vegetable oil for frying
Salt to taste

Creamed vegetable, chicken, eggs or
fish, if desired

━━━━━━━━━━ Coarsely grate potatoes. In a medium bowl, drop into cold water 5 to 10 minutes. Squeeze out moisture and pat dry with paper towels. Dip bird's nest baskets into hot oil to prevent sticking. Line larger basket with about ½-inch layer of potatoes. Clamp on smaller basket. Fry in hot oil 2 to 3 minutes or until crisp and golden. Drain. Let cool 2 to 3 minutes. Remove clamps and lift out smaller basket. Carefully unmold fried nest. Sprinkle with salt to taste. Fill with creamed vegetable, chicken, eggs or fish, if desired. Makes 6 to 8 nests.

Note:
Bird's nest baskets are available in gourmet shops and in the housewares section of some department stores.

Mini-Potato Puffs

A mini-potato with a maxi appeal! (Photo on page 63.)

½ cup water
½ cup milk
2 tablespoons butter or margarine
½ teaspoon salt

1⅓ cups dry instant mashed potatoes
2 eggs, slightly beaten
Vegetable oil for frying

In a medium saucepan, heat water, milk, butter or margarine and salt to boiling. Remove from heat and stir in dry instant potatoes. Cool about 10 minutes. Stir eggs into potato mixture. Refrigerate until cold, about 2 hours. Shape in 18 to 20 (1½-inch) balls. Place several puffs in raised fryer basket. Lower into hot oil and fry 1 to 2 minutes until golden brown. Makes 18 to 20 puffs.

Potato Puffs

Take time for these!

1½ lbs. potatoes
¼ cup dairy sour cream
2 eggs, slightly beaten
2 tablespoons chopped chives
1 tablespoon melted butter

½ teaspoon salt
½ cup all-purpose flour
½ cup milk
½ cup fine dry bread crumbs
Vegetable oil for frying

Peel potatoes and cut in quarters. In a large saucepan, cover potatoes with water and boil until tender. Drain thoroughly. Put through ricer or sieve. Add sour cream, 1 egg, chives, butter and salt. Stir to blend well. Chill 1 hour. With lightly floured hands, form in balls about 1½ inches in diameter. In a small bowl, coat balls with flour. Chill another 2 hours. In a small bowl, combine milk and 1 egg. Dip chilled potato balls in milk-egg mixture, then into bread crumbs. Place several balls in raised fryer basket. Lower into hot oil and fry until golden, about 1 minute. Drain. Bake in a 400°F (204°C) oven 4 minutes or until they puff slightly and crack. Makes 25 to 30 puffs.

Vegetables

The shapes and forms of fried vegetables seem endless. You can chop, slice, grate, dice, quarter, halve, or even fry some of them whole. After you get them in one of these shapes, you can marinate them in all kinds of seasonings, then coat them with flour, egg, crumbs, cornmeal or a batter made of a combination of ingredients.

You'll marvel at fried zucchini. Zucchini Sticks, page 102, have a coating of flour, egg and bread crumbs. You can use that same coating recipe and cut the zucchini in thin circles, long wedges or thick chunks. Each shape will have an entirely different look, yet the flavor remains the same. If you want still another variation on the zucchini theme, try Zucchini Fritters, page 102. They are grated, mixed into a batter, and dropped into hot oil in the deep-fryer.

When dropping food into the deep-fryer, drop it very carefully. The fryer basket can be placed in the lower position. For vegetable-fritter batters, drop by teaspoonfuls or tablespoonfuls, as indicated in the recipe. Hold the spoon with the uncooked fritter in it as close as possible to the hot oil. When it is brown on one side, turn it over with a metal slotted spoon or turner. Continue cooking on the other side until golden brown or for the time suggested in the recipe. Raise the basket and drain vegetables.

Most vegetables do not need to be pre-cooked before frying. Whole okra and fresh green beans are exceptions to this rule. They are more tender if simmered several minutes before being deep-fried.

Old-Fashioned French-Fried Onion Rings, page 95.

Fried Artichoke Hearts

Adds a gourmet touch to any menu.

1 (9-oz.) pkg. frozen artichoke hearts
1 egg
1 tablespoon water
¾ cup fine dry bread crumbs
¼ teaspoon salt

⅛ teaspoon pepper
¼ teaspoon garlic salt
⅛ teaspoon paprika
Vegetable oil for frying
Lemon wedges, if desired

⬛⬛⬛⬛⬛⬛ Partially thaw artichoke hearts. Pat dry with paper towels. In a small bowl, beat egg and water. In a shallow dish, combine bread crumbs, salt, pepper, garlic salt and paprika. Dip artichokes into egg mixture, then into bread crumbs. Using fryer basket, fry in hot oil 2 to 3 minutes or until brown and artichokes are done. Cooking time will vary with size of artichoke. Raise fryer basket, drain and serve hot with lemon wedges, if desired. Makes 4 servings.

French-Fried Asparagus

Crisp with a lacy look.

2 tablespoons all-purpose flour
2 tablespoons evaporated milk,
    undiluted
1 egg, beaten

1 lb. fresh asparagus
Vegetable oil for frying
Salt and pepper to taste

⬛⬛⬛⬛⬛⬛ In a small bowl, combine flour, evaporated milk and egg. Mix until smooth. Trim and wash asparagus. Drain and pat dry with paper towels. Cut each trimmed stalk in half. Dip into batter. Let excess batter drip into bowl. Using fryer basket, fry in hot oil about 1 minute or until coating is golden and crispy. Raise fryer basket, drain and sprinkle with salt and pepper to taste. Serve hot. Makes 4 to 6 servings.

See-Through Onion Rings

Just a scanty coating for these onions.

2 medium onions
½ cup evaporated milk, undiluted
½ cup all-purpose flour

Vegetable oil for frying
Salt to taste

⬛⬛⬛⬛⬛⬛ Peel onions and cut in ¼-inch slices. Separate in rings. In a small bowl, dip into milk, then in another bowl, dip slices into flour. Place several rings in raised fryer basket. Lower into hot oil and fry 2 minutes or until golden. Drain and sprinkle with salt to taste. Serve hot. Makes 4 servings.

Carrot Stacks

You'll never believe this terrific combination until you try it!

3 medium carrots, peeled
1 egg, slightly beaten
¼ teaspoon salt
1 teaspoon brown sugar

¼ teaspoon ground ginger
2 tablespoons all-purpose flour
Vegetable oil for frying

▬▬▬▬▬▬ Coarsely grate carrots. In a medium bowl, combine egg, salt, brown sugar, ginger and flour. Stir in grated carrots. Place fryer basket in lowered position. With a teaspoon, pile mixture on another teaspoon, pressing slightly to make mixture more compact so carrots will not separate in frying. Drop into hot oil. Fry about 2 minutes or until golden. Raise fryer basket, drain and serve hot. Makes 4 servings.

Corn Fritters

A favorite with chicken dinners!

1 (7-oz.) can whole-kernel corn
Milk
1½ cups all-purpose flour
1 tablespoon baking powder

¾ teaspoon salt
1 egg, beaten
Vegetable oil for frying
Maple syrup

▬▬▬▬▬▬ Drain corn, reserving liquid. Add enough milk to liquid to make 1 cup. In a medium bowl, stir together flour, baking powder and salt. In a small bowl, combine corn, milk mixture and egg. Stir into dry ingredients. Mix just until moistened. Place fryer basket in lowered position. Drop batter by heaping tablespoonfuls into hot oil. Fry 1 to 1½ minutes or until golden brown. Raise fryer basket, drain and serve hot with maple syrup. Makes 4 servings.

Cook cauliflower until tender but firm. Drain and place in a medium bowl. Pour salad dressing over cauliflower and let stand at least one hour to absorb flavors.

How to Make Marinated Cauliflower Fritters

Drain marinated cauliflower thoroughly. With tongs, dip into prepared batter. Let excess drip before frying.

After cauliflower fritters are fried in hot oil, sprinkle with grated Parmesan cheese.

Marinated Cauliflower Fritters

Marinate cauliflower ahead of time, then fry just before serving.

1 small head cauliflower
1 cup red wine vinegar and oil
  salad dressing
1 cup all-purpose flour
1 teaspoon baking powder

¼ teaspoon salt
1 egg, slightly beaten
¾ cup milk
Vegetable oil for frying
Grated Parmesan cheese

██████████████ Break cauliflower in flowerets. Cook in salted water until done but firm, about 8 minutes. Drain. In a medium bowl, pour salad dressing over cooked cauliflower. Marinate at least 1 hour. Drain thoroughly. In a small bowl, combine flour, baking powder and salt. Stir in egg and milk. Mix until almost smooth. Dip drained cauliflower into batter. Place fryer basket in lower position. Fry cauliflower in hot oil until golden brown. Raise fryer basket, drain and sprinkle with grated Parmesan cheese. Serve hot. Makes 4 servings.

Fried Carrot Nuggets

The true carrot flavor comes through with every bite.

6 medium carrots, peeled, cut in thirds
1 egg, slightly beaten
2 tablespoons milk

Fine dry bread crumbs
Vegetable oil for frying

██████████████ In a medium saucepan, cover carrots with water. Bring to a boil and simmer about 5 minutes or until almost done. Plunge carrots into cold water, then drain and pat dry with paper towels. In a shallow bowl, mix egg and milk. Dip carrots into egg-milk mixture, then into bread crumbs. Place fryer basket in lowered position. Fry carrots in hot oil about 2 minutes or until golden. Raise fryer basket and drain. Makes 4 servings.

Farmland Corn Fritters

Quick and delicious!

2 cups buttermilk baking mix
½ cup cold water
1 egg, slightly beaten
1 (17-oz.) can whole-kernel corn,
   drained

Vegetable oil for frying
Powdered sugar or maple syrup

■■■■■■ In a medium bowl, combine baking mix, cold water and egg until smooth. Add corn. Place fryer basket in lowered position. Drop batter by teaspoonfuls into hot oil. Fry about 2½ minutes or until golden brown and done in center. Raise fryer basket, drain and sprinkle with powdered sugar or serve with maple syrup. Makes about 2 dozen fritters.

Fresh Corn Fritters

Lighter than most corn fritters—with a bacon flavor.

1 cup fresh corn kernels, cut from
   1 large ear of corn
2 eggs, beaten
¼ cup all-purpose flour
½ teaspoon salt
⅛ teasoon pepper

1 slice bacon, cooked until crisp,
   crumbled
1 tablespoon finely chopped green
   onion
Vegetable oil for frying

■■■■■■ In a medium bowl, combine corn, eggs, flour, salt, pepper, crumbled bacon and green onion. Place fryer basket in lowered position. Carefully drop batter by tablespoonfuls into hot oil. Fry about 1 to 1½ minutes or until golden. Raise fryer basket, drain and serve hot. Makes 8 or 9 fritters.

French-Fried Parsley

A real conversation piece!

1 large bunch fresh parsley

Vegetable oil for frying

■■■■■■ Break off parsley stems from clusters of leaves. Wash and thoroughly dry. If necessary, wrap in paper towels and leave in refrigerator several hours. Place several pieces in raised fryer basket. Lower into hot oil and fry for just an instant until crisp. Parsley cooks very quickly so be careful not to overcook. Drain well. Use as a garnish for fried main dishes or vegetables.

Old-Fashioned French-Fried Onion Rings

Try this batter for French-fried zucchini or carrot slices. (Photo on page 89.)

1 egg	¼ teaspoon salt
1 cup milk	3 large onions
1 tablespoon vegetable oil	Vegetable oil for frying
1 cup all-purpose flour	Salt to taste, if desired
1 teaspoon baking powder	

■■■■■■■■ In a medium bowl, combine egg, milk and 1 tablespoon oil. Add flour, baking powder and ¼ teaspoon salt. Beat until smooth. Peel and slice onions in ¼-inch-thick crosswise slices; separate in rings. Dip rings into batter. Place fryer basket in lowered position. Carefully drop rings 1 at a time into hot oil and fry until golden. Raise fryer basket, drain and sprinkle with salt to taste, if desired. Serve hot. Makes 4 to 5 servings.

Fried Green-Pepper Rings

Serve as a vegetable or a garnish for roasts or steaks.

2 large green bell peppers	¼ teaspoon pepper
½ cup fine dry bread crumbs	2 eggs, beaten
¼ cup grated Parmesan cheese	¼ cup water
2 teaspoons salt	Vegetable oil for frying

■■■■■■■■ Remove seeds and center of bell peppers. Cut crosswise in ¼-inch rings. In a pie plate, coat rings with a mixture of bread crumbs, grated Parmesan cheese, salt and pepper. In a small bowl, dip rings into a mixture of egg and water. Coat again with bread crumb mixture. Chill 1 hour. Place fryer basket in lowered position. Carefully drop rings 1 at a time into hot oil and fry about 30 seconds or until golden brown. Raise fryer basket, drain and serve hot. Makes 4 servings.

Squash Drops

A new way to serve squash.

2 cups cooked mashed acorn or
   banana squash
1 egg, beaten
⅓ cup all-purpose flour

½ teaspoon baking powder
½ teaspoon salt
⅛ teaspoon ground nutmeg
Vegetable oil for frying

██████ In a medium bowl, mix cooked mashed squash, egg, flour, baking powder, salt and nutmeg. Place fryer basket in lowered position. Drop batter by teaspoonfuls into hot oil. Fry about 2 minutes or until brown. Raise fryer basket, drain and serve hot. Makes 4 servings.

Fried Sweet Potatoes

A change-of-pace potato dish!

2 medium sweet potatoes
Vegetable oil for frying
Salt to taste

Brown sugar, if desired
Grated nutmeg, if desired

██████ Peel sweet potatoes and cut in ¼-inch-crosswise slices. Place several slices into raised fryer basket. Lower into hot oil and fry 1½ to 2 minutes or until done. Raise fryer basket and drain on paper towels. Sprinkle lightly with salt to taste, then with brown sugar and nutmeg, if desired. Makes 4 servings.

Vegetables you can use to make delectable taste treats. Zucchini rounds made from Zucchini Sticks recipe, page 102, are in lower part of photo.

Corny Corn Balls

Corn plus cornmeal gives the extra flavor.

1 cup all-purpose flour
¼ cup cornmeal
2 teasoons baking powder
½ teaspoon baking soda
½ teaspoon salt

1 egg, beaten
¼ cup dairy sour cream
1 (7-oz.) can cream-style corn
Vegetable oil for frying
Honey

█████████ In a medium bowl, stir together flour, cornmeal, baking powder, baking soda and salt. Add egg, sour cream and corn. Stir until well-blended. Place fryer basket in lowered position. Drop batter by tablespoonfuls into hot oil. Fry 2½ to 3½ minutes or until golden brown. Raise fryer basket, drain and serve warm with honey. Makes 16 to 20 corn balls.

French-Fried Eggplant

Dip it into bread, cracker or corn flake crumbs.

1 medium eggplant, peeled
Salt
½ cup all-purpose flour
1 egg, slightly beaten

2 tablespoons milk
⅔ cup fine dry seasoned bread crumbs
Vegetable oil for frying

█████████ Cut eggplant in ½-inch-crosswise slices; halve each slice. Sprinkle with salt. In a shallow dish, dip eggplant into flour, then in a small bowl, dip each slice into egg mixed with milk and then dip into seasoned bread crumbs. Place several slices into raised fryer basket. Lower into hot oil and fry about 1 minute on each side or until golden brown and tender. Raise fryer basket, drain and serve hot. Makes 4 to 5 servings.

Fried Okra

A Southern tradition!

1 lb. whole okra, fresh or frozen	½ teaspoon salt
1 egg	⅛ teaspoon pepper
1 tablespoon water	Vegetable oil for frying
¾ cup fine cracker crumbs	Creole Sauce, page 150, if desired

In a medium saucepan, cover okra with water. Cover and simmer 5 minutes. Drain and pat dry with paper towels. In a small bowl, beat egg with water. In a shallow dish, combine cracker crumbs, salt and pepper. Dip okra into egg mixture, then into crumbs. Place fryer basket in lowered position. Fry in hot oil about 2 minutes or until golden brown. Raise fryer basket, drain and serve hot plain or with Creole Sauce, if desired. Makes 4 to 6 servings.

Heavenly Onion Rings

Beautiful every time—light and tender to eat.

2 medium onions	¼ teaspoon salt
1 egg	¼ teasoon seasoned salt
1 cup buttermilk	½ teaspoon baking soda
1 cup all-purpose flour	Vegetable oil for frying

Peel and slice onions ¼-inch thick. Separate in rings. In a medium bowl, beat egg with buttermilk. Stir in flour, salt, seasoned salt and baking soda until almost smooth. Dip onion rings into batter. Place fryer basket in lowered position. Fry in hot oil about 1 to 2 minutes or until crisp and golden. Raise fryer basket, drain and serve hot. Makes 3 to 4 servings.

Sweet-Potato Balls

A surprise in each center!

2 large cooked sweet potatoes (about
   2 cups)
¼ teaspoon salt
1 tablespoon brown sugar

6 large marshmallows, cut in half
¼ cup melted butter or margarine
½ cup dry bread crumbs
Vegetable oil for frying

████████████ Peel and mash cooked sweet potatoes. In a medium bowl, combine sweet potatoes, salt and brown sugar. Shape mixture in 12 balls around marshmallow halves. In a shallow dish, roll balls in melted butter or margarine, then roll in bread crumbs. Chill about 1 hour. Place several balls into raised fryer basket. Fry in hot oil 1½ to 2 minutes or until golden brown. Drain and serve hot. Makes 12 balls.

How to Make Sweet-Potato Balls

Place part of mixture in hand, top with marshmallow and spoon remaining mixture over all. Lightly press into round shape.

Roll filled sweet-potato balls in melted butter, then in bread crumbs. Fry until golden brown.

Rice & Cheese Balls

Italian influence!

½ cup uncooked long-grain rice
2 tablespoons butter or margarine
2 tablespoons finely chopped onion
½ teaspoon seasoned salt
¾ cup chicken broth or bouillon
¼ cup dry white wine

2 tablespoons grated Parmesan cheese
2 eggs, slightly beaten
1 oz. mozzarella cheese, cut in ½-inch
   cubes
Fine dry bread crumbs
Vegetable oil for frying

In a medium skillet, saute rice in butter or margarine several minutes. Stir in onion, seasoned salt, broth or bouillon and wine. Cover and simmer about 20 minutes or until rice is tender. Remove from heat. Immediately stir in grated Parmesan cheese. In a medium bowl, combine eggs and cooked rice mixture. Cover and refrigerate at least 1 hour. Scoop up 1 tablespoon of rice mixture in a spoon. Place a cube of mozzarella cheese in middle and then top with another spoonful of rice mixture. Press together to form a ball; if necessary, dip hands in bread crumbs to keep rice from sticking to them. Roll balls in bread crumbs. Place balls in raised fryer basket. Lower into hot oil and fry 1 minute or until golden brown. Drain and serve hot. Makes 10 balls.

Rice Fritters

A pleasant change from potatoes or plain rice.

1 cup all-purpose flour
1½ teaspoons baking powder
¼ teaspoon salt
1 egg, slightly beaten
1 cup cooked rice
½ cup milk

1 green onion, finely chopped
2 tablespoons melted butter or
   margarine
Vegetable oil for frying
Grated Parmesan cheese

In a small bowl, stir together flour, baking powder and salt. In a medium bowl, combine egg, cooked rice, milk, green onion and butter or margarine. Add dry ingredients to egg mixture, stirring just until flour is moistened. Place fryer basket in lowered position. Drop batter by heaping teaspoonfuls into hot oil. Fry about 1½ minutes on each side or until golden brown. Drain and sprinkle with grated Parmesan cheese while hot. Makes about 20 fritters.

Zucchini Fritters

They puff into a variety of different shapes.

1 cup all-purpose flour
1½ teaspoons baking powder
½ teaspoon salt
2 teaspoons sugar
2 egg yolks
⅓ cup milk

1 tablespoon melted butter or
  margarine
1 cup finely grated unpeeled zucchini
2 egg whites, stiffly beaten
Vegetable oil for frying
⅓ cup grated Parmesan cheese

████████ In a medium bowl, stir together flour, baking powder, salt and sugar. In a small bowl, beat egg yolks well; stir in milk and melted butter or margarine. Stir egg mixture into dry ingredients. Carefully fold in zucchini and beaten egg whites. Place fryer basket in lowered position. Drop batter by tablespoonfuls into hot oil. Fry about 1½ minutes on each side. Raise fryer basket, drain and shake 1 or 2 fritters at a time in a bag with grated Parmesan cheese. Serve hot. Makes 20 to 24 fritters.

Zucchini Sticks

Cut zucchini in thin rounds instead of sticks, if you prefer. (Photo on page 97.)

3 medium zucchini
3 tablespoons all-purpose flour
¼ teaspoon salt
⅛ teaspoon pepper
⅛ teaspoon garlic powder

2 eggs
2 tablespoons lemon juice
¾ cup fine dry bread crumbs
Vegetable oil for frying
Salt or seasoned salt to taste

████████ Cut zucchini in sticks about ½-inch thick. In a shallow dish, mix flour, salt, pepper and garlic powder. Roll zucchini in flour mixture. In a small bowl, beat eggs slightly with lemon juice. Dip flour-coated zucchini into egg mixture, then into bread crumbs. Place several sticks into raised fryer basket. Lower into hot oil and fry until golden brown. Raise fryer basket, drain and serve hot. Sprinkle with salt or seasoned salt to taste. Makes 4 servings.

Using a grater with fairly large holes, grate unpeeled zucchini.

How To Make Zucchini Fritters

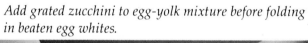

Add grated zucchini to egg-yolk mixture before folding in beaten egg whites.

Pour grated cheese into a small plastic bag; add one or two fritters. Shake bag to coat fritters.

Green-Bean Fritters

Don't be surprised if each one is a different shape.

1½ cups all-purpose flour
1 tablespoon baking powder
¾ teaspoon salt
1 egg, beaten
1 cup milk

1 (16-oz.) can cut green beans, thoroughly drained
Vegetable oil for frying
Seasoned salt to taste

In a medium bowl, combine flour, baking powder and salt. In a small bowl, combine egg, milk and green beans. Add to dry ingredients. Mix just until moistened. Place fryer basket in lowered position. Drop batter by tablespoonfuls into hot oil. Fry 3 to 4 minutes or until golden brown, turning once. Raise fryer basket, drain and sprinkle with seasoned salt to taste. Makes about 24 fritters.

Deviled Brussels Sprouts

Deviled Sauce gives a flavor lift to Brussels sprouts.

1 pint Brussels sprouts
1 egg, slightly beaten

Deviled Sauce:
2 tablespoons butter
1 teaspoon prepared mustard

¼ cup fine dry bread crumbs
Vegetable oil for frying

½ teaspoon Worcestershire sauce
1 tablespoon ketchup

Prepare Deviled Sauce. Trim and wash Brussels sprouts. Pat dry with paper towels. In a small bowl, dip Brussels sprouts into egg, then into bread crumbs. Place fryer basket in lowered position. Carefully drop Brussles sprouts into hot oil. Fry about 1 minute on each side or until brown and tender. Raise fryer basket and drain. Drizzle Deviled Sauce over hot Brussels sprouts. Serve hot. Makes 4 servings.

Deviled Sauce:
In a small saucpan, melt butter. Stir in mustard, Worcestershire sauce and ketchup. Cover and keep warm.

Mexican Corn Fritters

South-of-the-Border flavor.

3 tablespoons all-purpose flour
½ teaspoon baking powder
¼ teaspoon salt
¼ cup grated Parmesan cheese
1 egg, slightly beaten
1 cup drained corn, fresh, frozen or
   canned

1 tablespoon chopped pimiento
1 tablespoon chopped green onion
1 tablespoon chopped canned green
   chilies
Vegetable oil for frying

━━━━━━ In a medium bowl, combine flour, baking powder, salt and grated Parmesan cheese. Stir in egg, corn, pimiento, green onion and chilies. Place fryer basket in lowered position. Drop batter by heaping tablespoonfuls into hot oil. Fry about 1 minute on each side or until golden brown. Raise fryer basket, drain and serve hot. Makes 12 fritters.

Corn Puffs

A light and puffy fritter.

2 egg yolks
1 cup drained corn, fresh, frozen or
   canned
¼ teasoon salt
⅛ teaspoon pepper

2 tablespoons all-purpose flour
2 egg whites
Vegetable oil for frying
Honey or maple syrup, if desired

━━━━━━ In a medium bowl, beat egg yolks until light. Stir in corn, salt, pepper and flour. In a small bowl, beat egg whites until stiff but not dry. Fold into corn mixture. Place fryer basket in lowered position. Drop batter by tablespoonfuls into hot oil. Fry about 3 minutes or until golden brown. Raise fryer basket, drain and serve plain or with honey or maple syrup, if desired. Makes 14 puffs.

Breads

As a method for cooking bread, frying is traditional for many favorite regional or ethnic breads. Hush Puppies, page 111, are favorite in the South, Sopaipillas, page 114, are popular in the Southwest and Indian Fry-Bread, page 110, is a contribution from the American Indian. All of these plus many more are just right for your deep-fryer. The varieties range from quick breads to yeast breads, those made from a buttermilk baking mix to those from frozen bread dough.

Small size is the common denominator. Sopaipillas, which have been popular in the Southwest for years, are just becoming known in other parts of the country. They are made from small squares or rectangles of dough. When dropped into hot oil, they puff up and become hollow in the center. There's no waiting around for bread to rise or long baking times. In fact, there's no yeast in sopaipillas, just a mixture of flour, baking powder, salt and shortening with water stirred in. It's hard to believe that these ingredients, when combined and fried, could result in such marvelous golden puffs. Many people like to sprinkle sopaipillas with cinnamon and sugar and serve them instead of doughnuts, while others serve them as bread and pour honey over them or tear off a corner and pour honey inside.

Herb Puffs, page 115, are well worth the extra time it takes to make yeast rolls from scratch. They are light, puffy and delightfully herb flavored. Or try a short-cut to delicious fried bread with frozen bread dough. Garlic-Cheese Rolls, page 110, are aromatic with a surprisingly pleasant flavor. Even if you omit the garlic, they will make a hit with everyone.

Sopaipillas, page 114.

After adding other ingredients, stir enough flour into yeast mixture to make a stiff dough.

How To Make Fried Onion Buns

When dough has risen, break off a two-inch piece of dough for each bun.

With fingers, pat out each piece of dough in a three-inch round.

Fried Onion Buns

These savory buns are great with barbecued beef or ribs.

1 large onion, minced
3 tablespoons butter or margarine
¾ cup milk, scalded
1 teaspoon honey
½ teaspoon salt
½ teaspoon coarsely ground pepper

½ teaspoon celery salt
1 (¼-oz.) pkg. active dry yeast
   (1 tablespoon)
¼ cup warm water, (110°F/45°C)
2¾ to 3 cups all-purpose flour
Vegetable oil for frying

━━━━━━━━ In a small saucepan or skillet, saute onion in 1 tablespoon of butter or margarine. Place remaining 2 tablespoons butter or margarine in a medium bowl. Pour hot milk over butter or margarine. Add honey, salt, pepper and celery salt. Stir until butter or margarine melts. Cool to lukewarm. In a 1-cup measure, sprinkle yeast over warm water and stir until dissolved. Let stand in a warm place about 10 minutes. Stir sauteed onions and dissolved yeast mixture into lukewarm milk mixture. Add ½ of flour to milk mixture. Beat 3 minutes. With a spoon, stir in enough of remaining flour to make a stiff dough. Turn dough out on a lightly floured board. Knead about 5 minutes or until elastic. Place dough in a large buttered bowl and turn dough to butter top. Cover and let rise until doubled in bulk, about 1½ hours. Punch down. Separate dough in 2-inch pieces and pat out to 3-inch rounds. Place several pieces into raised fryer basket. Lower into hot oil and fry until golden brown. Drain and serve warm. Makes 1½ dozen buns.

Variation:

To make *Cream-Cheese Turnovers*, combine 2 ounces soft cream cheese, ¼ cup sour cream and 2 slices cooked crumbled bacon. Set aside. Follow directions for making onion buns, except separate dough in 1-inch pieces. On a lightly floured board, roll out dough pieces to 3-inch rounds. Spread about 2 teaspoons of cream-cheese filling over ½ of each round. Fold over to enclose filling. Pinch edges to seal. Fry in hot oil in until golden brown. Serve warm. Makes 30 to 35 small turnovers.

Onion Hush Puppies

Onion-flavored hush puppies may become a new tradition!

¾ cup cornmeal
½ cup all-purpose flour
¾ teaspoon baking soda
½ teaspoon salt

1 egg, beaten
½ cup buttermilk
⅓ cup finely chopped onion
Vegetable oil for frying

━━━━━━━━ In a medium bowl, combine cornmeal, flour, baking soda and salt. Add egg and buttermilk; mix well. Stir in onion. Place fryer basket in lowered position. Drop batter by teaspoonfuls into hot oil. Fry 2 to 2½ minutes or until golden brown. Drain and serve hot. Makes 18 to 20 hush puppies.

Deep-Fried Croutons

Use as a topping for soups or green salads.

4 slices bread
Vegetable oil for frying

Seasoned salt or herb seasoning

■■■■■■ Trim crust off bread. Cut bread in ½-inch cubes. Place ½ of cubes in raised fryer basket. Lower into hot oil and fry about 30 seconds or until golden brown, moving croutons around constantly with a slotted spoon. Raise fryer basket, drain and sprinkle with seasoned salt or herb seasoning. Makes about 2 cups.

Indian Fry-Bread

This resembles a miniature pita bread.

1 cup all-purpose flour
¾ teaspoon baking powder

⅓ cup plus 1 tablespoon milk
Vegetable oil for frying

■■■■■■ In a small bowl, mix flour, baking powder and milk. Form dough in a ball. On a lightly floured board, knead until smooth, about 3 to 4 minutes. Place dough in a medium bowl, cover and let rise 30 minutes. Divide dough in 8 equal parts and shape in balls. On a lightly floured board, roll each ball in a 3-inch round, keeping remaining balls covered so dough does not dry out. Place several pieces into raised fryer basket. Lower into hot oil and fry about 1 minute on each side until golden brown. Serve warm. Makes 8 fry-breads.

Garlic-Cheese Rolls

Tasting is believing!

1 (16-oz.) loaf frozen bread dough
Vegetable oil for frying
⅓ cup melted butter or margarine

1 clove garlic, mashed
½ cup grated Parmesan cheese

■■■■■■ Thaw bread according to package directions. On a lightly floured board, divide in 18 balls. Cover and let stand about 15 minutes. Roll out each ball to a 4-inch round. Fold in sides of dough, then roll up, pinching seams to seal. Place seam-side-down on lightly buttered baking sheets. Cover and let rise until amost doubled in bulk, about 1 to 1½ hours. Place several pieces into raised fryer basket. Lower into hot oil and fry 1½ to 2½ minutes or until brown. Drain. In a small bowl, combine butter or margarine and garlic. Dip warm rolls into garlic mixture, then into grated Parmesan cheese. Serve hot. Makes 18 rolls.

Hush Puppies

Corn-bread mixture goes great with fried fish.

1½ cups cornmeal
½ cup all-purpose flour
2 teaspoons baking powder
½ teaspoon salt

1 egg, slightly beaten
¾ cup milk
Vegetable oil for frying

In a medium bowl, combine cornmeal, flour, baking powder and salt. In a small bowl, mix egg and milk. Stir into dry ingredients until just moistened. Place fryer basket in lowered position. Drop batter by tablespoonfuls into hot oil. Fry about 2 minutes on each side or until golden brown. Raise fryer basket, drain and serve hot. Makes 14 to 16 hush puppies.

Puffy Health Bread

Good whole-wheat flavor!

1 cup whole-wheat flour
¼ teaspoon salt

½ cup plain yogurt
Vegetable oil for frying

In a medium bowl, mix whole-wheat flour, salt and yogurt until well-blended. Shape in 12 balls. On a lightly floured board, roll in 3½- to 4-inch rounds. Place several pieces into raised fry basket. Lower into hot oil and fry 1 to 1½ minutes or until puffy and brown. Drain and serve warm. Makes 12 rolls.

Fried Cracker Bread

Crisp and bubbly like Armenian cracker bread.

1 (¼-oz.) pkg. active dry yeast
  (1 tablespoon)
1½ cups warm water
½ teaspoon salt

About 4 cups all-purpose flour
¼ cup toasted sesame seeds
Vegetable oil for frying

In a large bowl, stir yeast into warm water until dissolved. Add salt and enough flour to make to make a stiff dough. Turn onto a lightly floured board and knead until smooth and elastic, about 8 to 10 minutes. Shape in ball, place in a large buttered bowl and turn dough to butter top. Cover and let rise in a warm place until doubled in bulk, about 1½ hours. Punch down and let rise again, about 30 minutes. Pinch off a ball of dough about 1½ inches in diameter and roll out to a 3-inch round on a lightly floured board sprinkled with sesame seeds. Place several pieces into raised fryer basket. Lower into hot oil and fry about 1 minute on each side. Drain and serve warm or cold. Makes about 25 breads.

Fried Biscuits

The Southern complement to chicken and gravy!

½ cup all-purpose flour
1 teaspoon baking powder
⅛ teaspoon salt
1 tablespoon butter or margarine,
   cut in bits

3 tablespoons milk
Vegetable oil for frying

In a medium bowl, combine flour, baking powder and salt. With a pastry blender or fork, cut in butter or margarine until mixture resembles coarse crumbs. Pour in milk and mix with fork. Shape dough in a ball. On a lightly floured board, roll out ¼-inch thick. Cut with a biscuit cutter. Place several pieces into raised fryer basket. Lower into hot oil and fry about 1 minute on each side or until evenly browned. Drain and serve hot. Makes 10 biscuits.

Crunchy Rounds

Crisp like a cracker—light and puffy like a hollow biscuit.

1½ cups all-purpose flour
½ cup cornmeal
¾ teaspoon salt
1½ teaspoons dry mustard
½ teaspoon baking soda

⅓ cup shortening
1 tablespoon prepared horseradish
⅓ cup sour cream
Vegetable oil for frying

In a medium bowl, combine flour, cornmeal, salt, dry mustard and baking soda. With a pastry blender or fork, cut in shortening and horseradish until mixture resembles coarse crumbs. Stir in sour cream. On a lightly floured board, knead dough several times. Roll out about ⅛-inch thick. Cut with a biscuit cutter. Place several pieces into raised fryer basket. Lower in hot oil and fry about 2 minutes or until puffy and golden. Drain and serve warm or cool. Makes 28 to 32 rounds.

Shortcut Hush Puppies

Good texture with popular cornmeal crunch.

1 cup buttermilk baking mix
1 cup cornmeal
1 teaspoon salt

1 egg, slightly beaten
¾ cup milk
Vegetable oil for frying

■■■■■■■■ In a medium bowl, combine baking mix, cornmeal, salt, egg and milk. Place fryer basket in lowered position. Drop batter by teaspoonfuls into hot oil. Fry 2 to 2½ minutes or until brown. Drain and serve hot. Makes 15 to 20 hush puppies.

Yam Buns

A conversation-starter for your next salad luncheon.

1 small yam or sweet potato, cooked, peeled
2 tablespoons butter or margarine, softened
½ cup milk, scalded
1 cup all-purpose flour
1 cup whole-wheat flour

½ cup brown sugar
½ teaspoon salt
2 teaspoons baking powder
½ teaspoon ground cinnamon
¼ teaspoon ground nutmeg
Vegetable oil for frying

■■■■■■■■ In a large bowl, mash yam or sweet potato and butter or margarine; stir in hot milk. In a medium bowl, combine flours, brown sugar, salt, baking powder, cinnamon and nutmeg. Stir into yam mixture. Mix well. Cover and refrigerate at least 1 hour. On a lightly floured board, pat out chilled dough about ⅛-inch thick. Cut with a floured biscuit cutter. Place several pieces into raised fryer basket. Lower into hot oil and fry 1½ to 2 minutes or until golden brown. Drain and serve warm. Makes 20 to 30 buns.

Sopaipillas

Little pillow-shaped puffs, so light they melt in your mouth. (Photo on page 107.)

1 cup all-purpose flour
1½ teaspoons baking powder
¼ teaspoon salt
1 tablespoon shortening

⅓ cup water
Vegetable oil for frying
Honey and butter, if desired
Cinnamon and sugar, if desired

■■■■■ In a medium bowl, stir together flour, baking powder and salt. With a pastry blender or fork, cut in shortening until mixture resembles cornmeal. Gradually add water, stirring with a fork. Turn out on lightly floured board. Knead in a smooth ball. Divide in half, let stand 10 minutes. Roll out each half to a 12″ x 10″ rectangle. Cut in 3″ x 2″ rectangles. Do not re-roll or patch dough. Place several pieces in raised fryer basket. Lower into hot oil and fry about 1 minute on each side or until golden. Drain and serve hot with honey and butter, if desired, or roll in a mixture of cinnamon and sugar, if desired. Makes 20 sopaipillas.

Buñuelos

Mexicans make this version of puffy fried bread.

2 cups all-purpose flour
2 teaspoons sugar
½ teaspoon baking powder
¼ teaspoon salt
1 egg

⅓ cup milk
2 tablespoons melted butter
Vegetable oil for frying
Cinnamon
Sugar

■■■■■ In a medium bowl, combine flour, sugar, baking powder and salt. Add egg, milk and melted butter. Mix to form a soft dough. On a lightly floured board, knead about 2 minutes or until smooth. Divide in 24 balls. Cover and let stand 30 minutes. Roll out to 3½- to 4-inch rounds. Place several pieces in raised fryer basket. Lower into hot oil and fry 1 to 1½ minutes or until golden brown and puffy. Drain and sprinkle with cinnamon and sugar. Serve warm. Makes 24 buñuelos.

Cinnamon Blossoms

You'll like this short-cut with refrigerated biscuits.

1 (8-oz.) pkg. refrigerated biscuits
Vegetable oil for frying

¼ cup sugar
¼ teaspoon ground cinnamon

██████████ Separate biscuits. With scissors, make 5 cuts at regular intervals almost to center of each biscuit. Place fryer basket in lowered position. Fry biscuits in hot oil 1 minute on each side or until golden brown. Drain and coat warm blossoms with a mixture of sugar and cinnamon. Serve warm or cold. Makes 10 blossoms.

Herb Puffs

Try these for your next salad luncheon.

1 (¼-oz.) pkg. active dry yeast
   (1 tablespoon)
¼ cup warm water (110°F/45°C)
⅓ cup milk
1 tablespoon sugar
¾ teaspoon salt
¼ teaspoon fines herbes

⅛ teaspoon dried dill weed
1 tablespoon shortening
1¾ to 2 cups all-purpose flour
1 egg
Vegetable oil for frying
Butter or margarine

██████████ In a small bowl, dissolve yeast in warm water. In a small saucepan, heat milk, sugar, salt, fines herbes, dill weed and shortening until shortening starts to melt. In a medium bowl, combine dissolved yeast, hot-milk mixture, ½ cup of flour and egg. Beat well. Stir in remaining flour to form a moderately stiff sticky dough. Place in a large buttered bowl, cover and let rise in a warm place until doubled in bulk, about 45 minutes. Punch down. On a lightly floured board, divide dough in 18 pieces; pat each in a 3-inch round. Let stand in a warm place 30 minutes. Using the fryer basket, carefully lower bread rounds into hot oil in deep-fryer. Fry 1½ to 2 minutes or until golden and puffy. Drain and serve warm with butter or margarine. Makes 18 puffs.

Desserts

Deep-fried desserts are great when you want something special to top off a memorable meal. For a really different idea, try Funnel Cakes, page 124, an updated version of the traditional Pennsylvania-Dutch dish. It is called funnel cake because you pour batter through a funnel into the hot oil. It takes the shape of your deep-fryer and has the appearance of a maze created by the crisscrossing pattern of the batter. After it is fried and drained, you can sprinkle it with powdered sugar or top it with strawberries or blueberries and sour cream.

Swedish Rosettes, page 130, are my favorite. They are so delicate, yet crisp and golden. It is necessary to have a rosette iron to make these shapes. These irons are available in gourmet shops and department, hardware and discount stores. Just heat the iron, dip into the batter and fry. Sprinkle with powdered sugar and you'll marvel at these party-pretty rosettes.

Fruits are very prominent in fried desserts. You can slice and coat them with various crumb mixtures or you can chop them and mix into a fritter batter.

Most fruits are rather juicy so it is important to pour off liquid, then pat dry with paper towels. This enables the coating to stick more securely and helps them fry properly.

When lowering fruit fritters into hot oil, be sure to use the approximate amount that is suggested in the recipe. If you make them too large, it is difficult to get them done in the center without being overcooked on the outside.

Fry several at a time to prevent crowding. Turn them over when golden on one side, although some will turn themselves. Raise the fryer basket and drain before removing.

Pineapple Rings, page 118.

Pineapple Rings

A delightful fruit dessert! (Photo on page 117.)

1 cup flour
2 eggs
1 teaspoon baking powder
½ teaspoon salt
½ cup milk
1 teaspoon vegetable oil

1 teaspoon grated orange peel
1 egg white
1 small fresh pineapple
Vegetable oil for frying
Apricot-Orange Sauce, page 151, if
   desired

▬▬▬▬▬▬ In a medium bowl, stir together flour, baking powder and salt. Add eggs, milk, 1 teaspoon oil and grated orange peel. Beat until smooth. In a small bowl, beat egg white until soft peaks form. Fold into batter. Cut top and bottom from pineapple and peel, if desired. Slice in ¼-inch-crosswise slices. Pat dry with paper towels. Dip pineapple slices into batter. Place several in raised fryer basket. Lower into hot oil and fry 1 to 1½ minutes or until golden brown. Drain and serve hot. Makes about 20 to 24 rings.

Traditional Banana Fritters

Serve banana fritters plain or with a fancy sauce!

4 bananas
1 tablespoon lemon juice
2 tablespoons sifted powdered sugar
½ cup buttermilk baking mix
1 tablespoon sugar

1 egg, slightly beaten
¼ cup milk
Vegetable oil for frying
Sifted powdered sugar
Maple syrup or fruit sauce, if desired

▬▬▬▬▬▬ Peel bananas; cut each in 4 chunks. Sprinkle with lemon juice, then 2 tablespoons powdered sugar. Set aside while making batter. In a small bowl, combine baking mix, sugar, egg and milk. Beat with a spoon or whisk until almost smooth. Dip banana chunks into batter. Place fryer basket in lowered position. Gently drop into hot oil. Fry 1 to 1½ minutes or until golden. Raise fryer basket, drain and sprinkle with powdered sugar. Serve warm with maple syrup or fruit sauce, if desired. Makes 16 fritters.

Brandied Banana Fritters

A grand finale to any special dinner.

4 bananas
3 tablespoons sifted powdered sugar
¼ cup brandy
1 teaspoon grated lemon peel
1 cup all-purpose flour
1 teaspoon baking powder
¼ teaspoon salt

1 egg, separated
⅔ cup milk
1 teaspoon melted butter
Vegetable oil for frying
Whipped cream, maple syrup or
   brandy sauce

▬▬▬▬▬▬ Peel bananas. Cut each in 4 crosswise pieces, then cut each piece in half lengthwise. In a small bowl, stir together powdered sugar, brandy and grated lemon peel. Pour over bananas and marinate about 30 minutes. In a small bowl, combine flour, baking powder and salt. In another small bowl, beat egg white until stiff. In a medium bowl, beat egg yolk until light yellow; stir in milk and melted butter. Stir in flour mixture, then 1 tablespoon of brandy mixture in which bananas are marinating. Fold in egg white. Drain bananas thoroughly; dip into batter. Place fryer basket in lowered position. Fry in hot oil 1 to 2 minutes or until golden brown. Drain and serve warm with whipped cream, maple syrup or brandy sauce. Makes 8 fritters.

Caribbean Banana Fritters

Yummy ginger-rum sauce!

3 bananas
½ cup plus 1 tablespoon sugar
⅛ teaspoon ground ginger
¼ cup rum
2 eggs, separated

⅔ cup milk
1 tablespoon melted butter
1 cup all-purpose flour
¼ teaspoon salt
Vegetable oil for frying

▬▬▬▬▬▬ Peel bananas. Cut each in 1-inch crosswise slices. Place in a medium bowl. Sprinkle with 1 tablespoon of sugar and ginger. Pour rum over all. Let stand about 30 minutes. Drain bananas, reserving marinade. In a large bowl, beat egg yolks until light yellow. Add milk and melted butter. Stir in flour and salt. Beat until smooth. In a small bowl, beat egg whites until stiff. Fold into batter. Dip well-drained bananas into batter. Place fryer basket in lowered position. Drop bananas into hot oil. Fry 1 to 2 minutes or until brown. Raise fryer basket and drain. In a small saucepan, combine reserved marinade and ½ cup of sugar. Heat until sugar dissolves. Brush hot cooked fritters with sauce and serve hot. Makes about 16 fritters.

Citrus Rings

Tangy lemon and sweet candied orange flavors make this a taste treat to remember!

3 tablespoons butter, melted
1 cup milk
½ (¼-oz.) pkg. active dry yeast
1 egg, separated
⅔ cup all-purpose flour
2 very ripe lemons

1 jar orange marmalade with whole
    orange slices
½ cup kirsch
Dash salt
Few drops lemon juice
Powdered sugar

▬▬▬▬▬▬ In a medium bowl, combine butter, milk and yeast until well mixed. Stir in egg yolk and flour. Let stand at least 1 hour. Discard both ends of lemons and cut lemons in thin slices. Remove whole orange slices from marmalade; reserve marmalade for another use. Place lemon and orange slices in a large bowl. Pour kirsch over citrus slices and let stand 1 hour. In a small bowl, beat egg white, salt and lemon juice until stiff. Gently fold egg white into yeast batter. Dip each citrus slice into batter. Place several into raised fryer basket. Lower into hot oil and fry until golden brown and fluffy. Drain, sprinkle with powdered sugar and serve hot. Makes about 24 appetizers.

Hawaiian Fruit-Balls

A treat from the tropics!

1 cup all-purpose flour
1 teaspoon baking powder
½ teaspoon salt
2 eggs
½ cup milk
1 teaspoon vegetable oil

1 teaspoon grated orange peel
½ cup canned sliced pineapple,
    well-drained, cut in small pieces
½ cup diced bananas
Vegetable oil for frying
1 cup flaked coconut

Glaze:
1 cup sifted powdered sugar
1½ tablespoons milk

▬▬▬▬▬▬ Prepare Glaze. In a medium bowl, stir together flour, baking powder and salt. Add eggs, milk and 1 teaspoon oil. Beat with a rotary beater until smooth. Stir in grated orange peel, pineapple and banana pieces. Place fryer basket in lowered position. Drop by tablespoonfuls into hot oil. Fry about 2 minutes or until golden. Drain and dip warm fruit balls into Glaze, then into coconut. Makes 22 to 24 balls.

Glaze:
In a small bowl, mix powdered sugar and 1½ tablespoons milk.

Citrus Rings, above.

Cherry Twists El Charro

A delightful dessert inspired by Tucson, Arizona's El Charro Restaurant.

1 (20-oz.) can cherry or berry pie filling
1 egg, slightly beaten
1 tablespoon water

Vegetable oil for frying
Sifted powdered sugar

Basic Crepes:
4 eggs
¼ teaspoon salt
2 cups all-purpose flour

2¼ cups milk
2 tablespoons melted butter

Prepare Basic Crepes. Place 1 tablespoon of pie filling on lower third of each crepe. Brush bottom and top edges of crepe with egg mixed with water. Fold right and left sides of crepe over filling, then roll up. Place several crepes (seam side down) in raised fryer basket. Lower into hot oil and fry about 1 minute or until crisp and golden. Drain and sprinkle with powdered sugar. Spoon extra filling over top. Makes 10 to 12 cherry crepes.

Basic Crepes:
In a medium bowl, combine eggs and salt. Gradually add flour alternately with milk; beat with an electric mixer or whisk until smooth. Beat in melted butter. If blender is used, combine ingredients in blender jar and blend about 1 minute. Scrape down sides with a rubber spatula and blend for another 15 seconds. If possible, let stand 1 hour. Cook on upside-down crepe griddle or in a traditional crepe pan. Freeze extra crepes for future use. Makes 30 to 35 crepes.

Variation:
Substitute flour tortillas for crepes, using a wedge-shaped portion of tortilla. Substitute apples or other fruits for filling and add a dollop of whipped cream as a topping. Sprinkle cinnamon on top of whipped cream.

Cherry Twists El Charro, above.

Funnel Cakes

Amaze them all when you make this maze!

1 egg
¾ cup milk
1¼ cups all-purpose flour
2 tablespoons sugar
1 teaspoon baking soda
¾ teaspoon baking powder

¼ teaspoon salt
Vegetable oil for frying
Sifted powdered sugar
Strawberries, blueberries or maple
  syrup, if desired

———— In a medium bowl, beat egg, milk, flour, sugar, baking soda, baking powder and salt. Using a funnel with about a ⅜-inch-diameter spout opening, hold finger over end of funnel spout. Pour about 1 cup of batter into funnel. Hold funnel above deep-fryer and remove finger. As batter flows through spout, move funnel in a crisscrossing pattern above surface of hot oil until funnel is empty. Batter should drip rapidly through funnel spout; if too thick, add 1 to 1½ tablespoons milk. Cake will take shape of deep-fryer. Fry about 1 minute. Using 2 spatulas, turn and fry about 30 seconds. Drain and sprinkle with powdered sugar. Serve warm plain or with strawberries, blueberries or maple syrup, if desired. Makes 4 to 6 servings.

Hold your finger over the end of the funnel while pouring the batter into the top of the funnel. Remove your finger while moving the funnel in a crisscross pattern above the surface of the oil.

Keep funnel moving as batter will brown quickly. Use a metal spatula to turn the funnel cake so that the other side is browned. A cooked funnel cake will look like a curly golden maze.

Ambrosia Fritters

Texture like a delicate orange-coconut cake.

1 egg
¼ cup sugar
1 teaspoon grated orange peel
1 tablespoon shortening
1 cup all-purpose flour

1 teaspoon baking powder
¼ teaspoon salt
¼ cup orange juice
⅓ cup flaked coconut
Vegetable oil for frying

Orange Glaze:
1 cup sifted powdered sugar

2 tablespoons orange liqueur

████████████ Prepare Orange Glaze. In a medium bowl, beat egg until light and foamy. Beat in sugar, grated orange peel and shortening. In a small bowl, combine flour, baking powder and salt alternately with orange juice. Add flour mixture to egg mixture. Stir in coconut. Place fryer basket in lowered position. Drop by teaspoonfuls into hot oil. Fry 2 to 3 minutes or until brown. Raise fryer basket, drain and dip into Orange Glaze while warm. Makes 14 fritters.

Orange Glaze:
In a small bowl, combine powdered sugar with orange liqueur. Blend well.

Crunchy Strawberry Surprise

Crunchy on the outside, juicy on the inside!

½ cup apricot jam or preserves
1 pt. fresh strawberries
½ cup ground walnuts
2 eggs, slightly beaten

½ cup finely crushed vanilla wafers
Vegetable oil for frying
Sifted powdered sugar

████████████ Press jam or preserves through sieve into a small bowl. Wash and hull strawberries. If berries with long stems are available, do not hull, but dip in coatings by stems. Carefully pat strawberries dry with paper towels. Dip into preserves, using a fork to help completely coat berries. Allow excess to drip through fork tines. Coat with nuts. Shake gently. In another small bowl, dip berries into beaten eggs, smoothing off excess. Coat berries with crushed vanilla wafers. Place on a wire rack. Chill 30 minutes to set coating. Place fryer basket in lowered position. Carefully drop berries into hot oil. Fry until golden brown. Raise fryer basket, drain and sprinkle with powdered sugar. Serve as soon as berries have cooled enough to eat. Makes 15 to 25 strawberries, depending on size.

Fig Nut Won Ton

A different shortcut dessert.

½ cup chopped dried figs
¼ cup chopped walnuts
1 tablespoon lemon juice
½ teaspoon grated lemon peel

15 won ton skins or wrappers
Vegetable oil for frying
Sifted powdered sugar

▬▬▬▬▬▬▬ In a small bowl, combine figs, walnuts, lemon juice and grated lemon peel. Place about 1 rounded teaspoon of mixture in center of each won ton skin. Moisten edges of skin. Fold 2 opposite corners together, forming a triangle. Seal edges. Pull the right and left corners of folded triangle down and below folded edge so they slightly overlap. Moisten overlaping corners and pinch together. Place several won ton into raised fryer basket. Lower into hot oil and fry about 1 minute or until crisp and golden. Drain and sprinkle with powdered sugar. Serve warm or cool. Makes 15 won ton.

Note:
Won ton skins or wrappers are available in oriental markets, gourmet shops and the frozen-food or deli sections of many supermarkets.

Blintzes With Wine-Berry Sauce

Freeze crepes ahead and make these in a jiffy!

1 cup *dry* cottage cheese
1 (3-oz.) pkg. cream cheese, softened
½ teaspoon grated lemon peel
2 tablespoons sugar

8 to 10 Basic Crepes, page 122
1 egg
1 tablespoon water
Vegetable oil for frying

Wine-Berry Sauce:
1 cup seedless raspberry or
   blackberry preserves

1 teaspoon lemon juice
2 tablespoons port wine

▬▬▬▬▬▬▬ Prepare Wine-Berry Sauce. In a small bowl, combine dry cottage cheese, cream cheese, grated lemon peel and sugar. Mix thoroughly. Place about 2 tablespoons of mixture in center of each crepe. Brush edges of crepe with egg beaten with water. Fold over bottom, both sides and top. Place several blintzes in raised fryer basket. Lower into hot oil and fry 1 to 1½ minutes or until crisp and golden. Drain and serve warm with Wine-Berry Sauce. Makes 8 to 10 blintzes.

Wine-Berry Sauce:
In a small saucepan, heat preserves with lemon juice until mixture bubbles. Stir in wine. Cover and keep warm.

Date Won Ton

A great dessert that's not too sweet.

1 cup chopped dates
2 tablespoons crunchy peanut butter
2 teaspoons grated orange peel

18 won ton skins or wrappers
Vegetable oil for frying
Sifted powdered sugar

██████████ In a small bowl, mix dates, peanut butter and grated orange peel. Place about 1 rounded teaspoon of filling in center of each won ton skin. Moisten edges of skin. Fold 2 opposite corners together, forming a triangle. Seal edges. Pull right and left corners of folded triangle down and below folded edge so they slightly overlap. Moisten overlapping corners and pinch together. Place several won ton into raised fryer basket. Lower into hot oil and fry about 1 minute or until crisp and golden. Drain and sprinkle with powdered sugar. Makes 18 won ton.

Note:
Won ton skins or wrappers are available in oriental markets, gourmet shops and the frozen food or deli sections of many supermarkets.

French Fried Strawberries

Let everyone dip their own strawberries!

1 pt. fresh strawberries
1 egg, beaten
½ cup milk
2 tablespoons sugar
½ teaspoon baking powder
1 teaspoon melted butter or margarine

½ teaspoon vanilla extract
¾ cup all-purpose flour
Vegetable oil for frying
⅓ cup dairy sour cream
⅓ cup flaked coconut

██████████ Wash and hull strawberries. Gently pat dry with paper towels. In a small bowl, combine egg and milk. Stir in sugar, baking powder, butter or margarine, vanilla and flour. Beat until smooth. Spear berries with fondue forks or skewers and dip into batter. Fry in hot oil until golden. Drain and serve as soon as berries have cooled enough to eat. Dip into sour cream, then coconut. Makes 15 to 25 strawberries, depending on size.

Soufflé Fritters

The ultimate in elegant desserts!

¼ cup butter
½ cup water
½ cup all-purpose flour
2 eggs

1 tablespoon brandy or orange liqueur
Vegetable oil for frying
Sifted powdered sugar

Raspberry Sauce:
1 (10-oz.) pkg. frozen raspberries
1 tablespoon sugar

2 tablespoons cornstarch
2 tablespoons port wine

▬▬▬▬▬▬ In a medium saucepan, heat butter and water until butter melts and mixture boils. Remove from heat. Add flour all at once and beat vigorously with a wooden spoon until well-blended. Return pan to medium heat, beating constantly, about 1 minute or until mixture clings to spoon from bottom and sides of pan. Remove from heat and let stand 5 to 6 minutes. Meanwhile, prepare Raspberry Sauce. Make a well in center of dough. Drop in 1 egg and beat vigorously. Beat in remaining egg until smooth and glossy. Stir in brandy or orange liqueur. Place fryer basket in lowered position. Drop batter by teaspoonfuls into hot oil. Fry 4 to 5 minutes or until very puffy and brown. Drain and sprinkle with powdered sugar. Serve immediately with Raspberry Sauce. Makes about 10 to 12 fritters.

Raspberry Sauce:
Partially thaw raspberries. In a small saucepan, combine sugar and cornstarch. Stir in raspberries with juice. Cook over low heat, stirring until thick. Remove from heat. Stir in wine. Blend well and cover to keep warm.

Blueberry Fritters

A light batter, dotted with blueberries.

2 tablespoons sugar
1 cup frozen blueberries
1 cup all-purpose flour
1 teaspoon baking powder
¼ teaspoon ground nutmeg
¼ teaspoon grated orange peel

¼ teaspoon salt
1 egg, slightly beaten
¼ cup milk
Vegetable oil for frying
Sifted powdered sugar

▬▬▬▬▬▬ Sprinkle sugar over frozen berries. Let stand 1 hour. Drain well. In a medium bowl, mix flour, baking powder, nutmeg, grated orange peel and salt. Beat in egg and milk until smooth. Carefully fold in drained berries. Place fryer basket in lowered position. Drop batter by tablespoonfuls into hot oil. Fry 2 to 2½ minutes or until golden brown and done inside. Raise fryer basket, drain and sprinkle generously with powdered sugar. Serve warm. Makes 12 to 14 fritters.

Swedish Rosettes

A rosette iron makes these delicate party treats.

1 egg
1 tablespoon sugar
½ cup milk
½ cup all-purpose flour

¼ teaspoon salt
1 teaspoon vanilla extract
Vegetable oil for frying
Sifted powdered sugar

In a medium bowl, beat egg. Add sugar and milk. Stir in flour and salt and beat until smooth. Stir in vanilla. Heat rosette iron by dipping it into hot oil in deep-fryer. Quickly drain excess oil on paper towels so iron stays hot. Immediately dip iron into batter to not more than ¾ the depth of rosette iron. If only a thin layer adheres to rosette iron, dip again immediately. Plunge batter-coated iron into hot oil. Fry until active bubbling ceases. With a fork, ease rosette off iron onto paper towels. While warm, sprinkle with powdered sugar. Makes 2 to 3 dozen rosettes.

Note:
Rosette irons are available with other kitchen utensils in department stores, gourmet shops, hardware and discount stores.

How to Make Swedish Rosettes

Dip preheated rosette iron in batter immediately after heating it in oil. Do not immerse more than three-fourths the depth of the rosette iron. Plunge batter-coated iron into hot oil. Remove when rosette is golden.

Hold fried rosette over several layers of paper towels. Sometimes rosettes will fall off. If not, ease off with fork. Sprinkle with powdered sugar while warm.

Ricotta Puffs

Serve as a snack, dessert or even for breakfast.

½ **cup ricotta cheese**
2 **eggs**
2 **tablespoons sugar**
½ **cup all-purpose flour**
2 **teaspoons baking powder**

⅛ **teaspoon salt**
Vegetable oil for frying
Sifted powdered sugar
Jam or jelly, if desired

In a medium bowl, beat cheese, eggs and sugar with a wooden spoon until smooth. In a small bowl, stir together flour, baking powder and salt. Beat flour mixture into cheese mixture to form a smooth thick batter. Place fryer basket in lowered position. Drop batter by rounded teaspoonfuls into hot oil. Fry until golden brown, about 1 minute on each side. Raise fryer basket and drain. Just before serving, sift powdered sugar over top. Serve warm plain or with jam or jelly, if desired. Makes 16 to 18 puffs.

Greek Honey Puffs

Light and delicate in texture and flavor.

¾ **cup plain yogurt**
½ **teaspoon grated lemon peel**
1 **egg, separated**
1 **tablespoon melted butter**
1 **cup all-purpose flour**

2 **tablespoons sugar**
1 **teaspoon baking powder**
½ **teaspoon baking soda**
¼ **teaspoon salt**
Honey

In a medium bowl, mix yogurt, grated lemon peel, egg yolk and butter. Stir in flour, sugar, baking powder, baking soda and salt. In a small bowl, beat egg white until stiff but not dry. Fold into yogurt mixture. Place fryer basket in lowered position. Drop batter by teaspoonfuls into hot oil. Fry about 2 minutes or until golden brown. Raise fryer basket, drain and serve warm with honey. Makes 20 to 25 puffs.

Apple Rings

You might like these spicy rings better than apple pie.

2 large cooking apples
1 cup all-purpose flour
½ cup plus 2 tablespoons sugar
1 teaspoon baking powder
Dash salt

1 egg, beaten
1 teaspoon vegetable oil
⅔ cup milk
Vegetable oil for frying
½ teaspoon ground cinnamon

■■■■■■■ Core, peel and slice apples in rings about ¼-inch thick. In a medium bowl, thoroughly mix flour, 2 tablespoons of sugar, baking powder and salt. Combine egg, 1 teaspoon oil and milk; add, all at once, to dry ingredients, stirring just until blended. Dip apple rings into batter, 1 at a time. Place fryer basket in lowered position. Gently drop 1 ring at a time into hot oil and fry about 1 minute on each side. Drain and serve warm. Sprinkle warm rings with a mixture of ¼ cup of sugar and cinnamon, if desired. Makes 4 to 5 servings.

Fried Cinnamon Buns

Sugar and spice—that's what these buns are made of.

¾ cup milk
1 cup sugar
1 teaspoon salt
¼ cup butter or margarine
¼ cup warm water (110°F/45°C)
1 (¼-oz.) pkg. active dry yeast
   (1 tablespoon)

1 egg, beaten
3 to 3½ cups flour
1 teaspoon ground cinnamon
Vegetable oil for frying

■■■■■■■ In a small saucepan, combine milk, ¼ cup of sugar, salt and butter or margarine. Heat until butter or margarine begins to melt. Cool to lukewarm. Mix warm water and dry yeast; stir to dissolve. In a large bowl, combine dissolved yeast mixture with milk mixture, egg and 1½ cups of flour. Beat until smooth. Add more flour to make dough stiff. Knead on a lightly floured board until smooth and elastic, about 6 to 8 minutes. Place in a lightly buttered bowl, turn dough to butter top. Cover and let rise in a warm place until doubled in bulk, about 1 hour. Butter 2 baking sheets. Combine ¾ cup of sugar and cinnamon. Punch down dough and divide in half. Roll out each half to a 14" x 9" rectangle. Sprinkle each with ½ of sugar-cinnamon mixture. Roll up tightly to form 2 (9-inch) rolls. Press to seal seam. Cut each roll crosswise into 9 equal pieces. Place on a buttered baking sheet, cut side up. Press down lightly to flatten rolls. Cover and let rise in a warm place until doubled in bulk, about 30 minutes. Place several rolls into raised fryer basket. Lower into hot oil and fry 2 to 3 minutes or until golden brown. If some of sugar-cinnamon mixture oozes out into oil, scoop it off oil surface with a long spoon. Any remaining will solidify when oil cools and can be strained out. Makes 18 buns.

Apple Rings, above.

Apple Fritters

Great with a cup of coffee or glass of milk!

1 cup all-purpose flour
1 teaspoon baking powder
¼ teaspoon ground nutmeg
½ teaspoon salt
½ cup plus 2 tablespoons sugar

2 eggs
⅓ cup milk
1 large cooking apple, peeled, chopped
Vegetable oil for frying
1 teaspoon ground cinnamon

██████████ In a medium bowl, combine flour, baking powder, nutmeg, salt and 2 tablespoons of sugar. Add eggs and milk. Beat with a rotary beater until smooth. Stir in apples. Place fryer basket in lowered position. Drop batter by tablespoonfuls into hot oil. Fry 2½ to 3 minutes or until brown and done inside. Drain. While warm, roll in a mixture of ½ cup of sugar and cinnamon. Makes about 18 fritters.

Apple-Spice Rings

These rings have a spicy surprise inside!

2 cooking apples
¾ cup all-purpose flour
3 tablespoons sugar
⅛ teaspoon salt

1 egg, separated
¼ cup milk
½ teaspoon ground cinnamon
Vegetable oil for frying

██████████ Core and peel apples. Slice in rings ¼- to ⅓-inch thick. In a medium bowl, stir together flour, 1 tablespoon of sugar and salt. In a small bowl, beat together egg yolk and milk. In another small bowl, beat egg white until stiff. Stir egg-yolk mixture into dry ingredients, mixing until smooth. Fold egg white into mixture. In a shallow dish, combine 2 tablespoons of sugar and cinnamon. Dip apple rings into cinnamon-sugar mixture, then into batter, coating thoroughly. Place fryer basket in lowered position. Carefully drop apple rings into hot oil and fry 3 to 4 minutes or until golden brown and apples are done. Raise fryer basket, drain and serve warm. Makes 4 to 5 servings.

Knotted Pastry Ribbons

The shape is intriguing, yet simple.

1½ cups all-purpose flour
¼ cup vegetable oil
1 tablespoon sugar
1 egg

1 tablespoon dry white wine
¼ teaspoon salt
Vegetable oil for frying
Sifted powdered sugar

In a medium bowl, combine flour, ¼ cup oil, sugar, egg, wine and salt. On a lightly floured board, knead into a smooth dough. Cover and let stand 20 minutes. Knead again 1 to 2 minutes. Roll out ⅛-inch thick. Cut in strips about ½ inch wide and 5 inches long. Tie each strip loosely in a simple knot. Place fryer basket in lowered position. Fry in hot oil until golden, about 1 to 1½ minutes. Drain and sprinkle with powdered sugar. Serve warm or cold. Makes about 40 ribbons.

Butterfly Cookies

Twisted dough gives a butterfly effect.

3 egg yolks, slightly beaten
½ teaspoon salt
1 tablespoon sugar
½ teaspoon rum

½ cup all-purpose flour
Vegetable oil for frying
Sifted powdered sugar

In a medium bowl, mix egg yolks, salt, sugar, rum and flour. Turn out on a lightly floured board, working in a little more flour if needed to make a stiff dough. Knead until smooth, about 10 minutes. Roll out in 1 or 2 sheets about ¹⁄₁₆-inch thick. Cut in strips about 3″ x 2½.″ Make 3 gashes about 1½-inches long nearly to ends. Put 1 end through center gash and give it a twist to make a butterfly appearance. Place fryer basket in lowered position. Fry in hot oil until light brown. Drain and sprinkle with powdered sugar. Makes 15 to 20 cookies.

Rosy Cinnamon-Apple Rings

You'll want to try this with fresh pears, too!

1 egg, slightly beaten
1 cup milk
1 tablespoon vegetable oil
1 tablespoon sugar
1 cup all-purpose flour

1 teaspoon baking powder
¼ teaspoon salt
2 large cooking apples
Vegetable oil for frying

Cinnamon Sauce:
1 cup water
¼ cup sugar

2 teaspoon cornstarch
¼ cup red cinnamon candies

▬▬▬▬▬ Prepare Cinnamon Sauce. In a medium bowl, combine egg, milk and 1 tablespoon oil. Add sugar, flour, baking powder and salt. Beat until smooth. Core, peel and slice apples in rings about ¼-inch thick. Dip rings into batter, 1 at a time. Place fryer basket in lowered position. Gently drop each ring into hot oil and fry about 1 minute on each side. Drain. Serve warm with Cinnamon Sauce. Makes 4 servings.

Cinnamon Sauce:

In a small saucepan, combine water, sugar and cornstarch. Bring to a boil. Spoon in candies; stir until melted. Cover and keep warm.

After sauce for apples is thickened, spoon in cinnamon candies; stir until melted.

How to Make
Rosy Cinnamon-Apple Rings

To make apple rings, core and peel apples; slice crosswise into one-fourth-inch-thick rings.

Dip rings into batter; fry until golden. Pour warm cinnamon sauce over rings.

Dutch Apple Turnovers

Enjoy these with a large glass of cold milk.

2 cups all-purpose flour
½ teaspoon salt
1 teaspoon baking powder
½ cup milk

1 egg
¼ cup butter or margarine, melted
Vegetable oil for frying

Apple Filling:
3 medium apples
½ cup water
¼ cup dark-brown sugar

2 tablespoons butter or margarine
¼ teaspoon ground cinnamon

In a medium bowl, stir together flour, salt and baking powder. In a small bowl, beat milk and egg; stir into flour mixture. Stir in melted butter or margarine; dough will be soft. Turn dough out onto a lightly floured board. Knead about 4 minutes or until smooth. Shape in a ball. Place in a bowl, cover and refrigerate 30 minutes. Meanwhile, prepare Apple Filling. Divide dough in half. On lightly floured board, roll out 1 piece of dough about ⅛ inch thick. Cut in 4-inch squares. Place 2 tablespoons of filling in center of each square. Moisten edges and fold dough over filling to form triangles. Press edges to seal securely. Repeat with remaining piece of dough and filling. Place several in raised fryer basket. Lower into hot oil and fry about 1 minute or until brown on both sides. Drain and serve warm. Makes about 10 turnovers.

Apple Filling:
Peel, core and thinly slice apples. In a medium saucepan, combine sliced apples and water. Cook, stirring occasionally, over medium heat about 15 minutes or until apples are very soft. Stir in brown sugar, butter or margarine and cinnamon. Cook 3 to 5 minutes or until brown sugar dissolves.

Dutch Apple Turnovers, above.

Fried Twists

A not-so-sweet snack or dessert.

2 egg yolks
¼ cup milk
1 teaspoon grated lemon peel
1 egg white

1¾ cups buttermilk baking mix
Vegetable oil for frying
Sifted powdered sugar

In a medium bowl, beat egg yolks, milk and grated lemon peel. In a small bowl, beat egg white until stiff but not dry; fold into yolk mixture. Stir in baking mix. On a lightly floured board, roll out ½ of dough at a time ¹⁄₁₆-inch thick. Cut in 5″ x 2″ rectangles. Make a lengthwise slit 1 inch long in center of rectangle. Slip 1 end of dough through slit, forming a twist knot. Place fryer basket in lowered position. Fry in hot oil about 1 minute on each side or until golden. Drain and sprinkle with powdered sugar. Makes 24 twists.

Fried Ice Cream

A dramatic surprise for your guests. Impressive with any ice cream!

1 pint vanilla ice cream
2 eggs, beaten slightly
2 tablespoons milk
1½ cups finely crushed corn flakes
    (about 3 ounces)

⅛ teaspoon ground cinnamon
Vegetable oil for frying

With an ice cream scoop, form ice cream in 4 smooth balls. Immediately return to freezer on a shallow tray. Freeze several hours or until firm. In a medium bowl, combine eggs and milk. In another medium bowl, combine crushed corn flakes and cinnamon. Quickly dip firm ice cream into egg mixture, then into crumbs. Return to freezer. When firmly frozen, dip into egg mixture, then into crumbs again. Repeat a third time; freeze overnight or until very firm. Place 2 pieces at a time in raised fryer basket. Lower into hot oil and fry 45 to 60 seconds. Drain on paper towels a few seconds. Serve immediately. Makes 4 servings.

Pronto Date Rolls

Crescent rolls are a welcome short-cut.

1 (8-oz.) can refrigerated crescent rolls
16 whole pitted dates
¼ cup sugar

¼ teaspoon ground cinnamon
Vegetable oil for frying

■■■■■■■■■ Separate crescent dough in 8 triangles. Cut each in half, crosswise, forming 16 triangles. Place a date on each triangle. Fold wide-angled corner over date and roll to opposite edge. Seal dough at ends of roll. Place several rolls into raised fryer basket. Lower into hot oil and fry until deep golden brown. Drain and roll in a mixture of cinnamon and sugar. Makes 16 rolls.

Cottage-Cheese Puffs

Loaded with protein!

¾ cup cottage cheese
1 egg
¼ cup milk
½ teaspoon vanilla extract
¾ cup all-purpose flour

1½ teaspoons baking powder
½ teaspoon salt
Vegetable oil for frying
Sifted powdered sugar, if desired
Grape or berry jelly

■■■■■■■■■ In a medium bowl, beat cottage cheese and egg with a fork or whisk until well-blended. Beat in milk and vanilla. In a small bowl, mix together flour, baking powder and salt. Stir into cottage cheese mixture until blended. Place fryer basket in lowered position. Drop batter by rounded teaspoonfuls into hot oil. Fry until golden, about 2 to 3 minutes. Drain and sprinkle with powdered sugar, if desired. Serve warm with jelly. Makes 20 to 30 puffs.

Churros

So delicate and crisp, they look like ruffled ribbons.

¼ cup water
1/16 teaspoon salt
¼ teaspoon sugar
2 tablespoons butter or margarine
¼ cup all-purpose flour

1 egg
¼ teaspoon vanilla extract
Vegetable oil for frying
Sifted powdered sugar

▬▬▬▬ In a medium saucepan, combine water, salt, sugar and butter or margarine. Heat until butter or margarine melts. Bring to a full boil over medium-high heat. Add flour all at once. Remove from heat and beat with a spoon until it forms a thick paste that separates from sides of pan. Add egg, beating until smooth and shiny. Stir in vanilla. Let cool 15 minutes. Fill a large pastry bag or cookie press fitted with large star tip with ½ of mixture. Squeeze mixture into hot oil in deep-fryer to form a ribbon 4 to 5 inches long. Cut off with a knife. Fry until golden brown. Repeat with remaining dough. Drain and sprinkle with powdered sugar. Serve warm. Makes 22 to 25 churros.

Variation:
Slightly crush 1 teaspoon anise seed and combine with ½ cup sifted powdered sugar. Cover and let stand several hours. Sift and discard seeds. Sprinkle on hot churros.

Fried Cream

A creamy custard flavored center coated with crunchy almonds.

¼ cup sugar
⅛ teaspoon salt
¼ cup cornstarch
3 egg yolks, beaten slightly
2 cups milk
1 cinnamon stick
1 tablespoon rum

½ cup slivered almonds
  (about 2½ ounces)
1 whole egg
1 egg white
1¼ cups sugar cookie crumbs
  (8 (2¾-inch) cookies)
Vegetable oil for frying

▬▬▬▬ Line a 9" x 5" loaf pan with foil. Butter foil; set aside. In a medium saucepan, combine sugar, salt and cornstarch. Stir in 3 egg yolks and milk. Add cinnamon stick. Cook and stir over low heat until thick. Remove from heat; discard cinnamon stick. Stir in rum. Pour into prepared pan; spread evenly with a spatula or back of a large spoon. Refrigerate several hours or until firm. Finely grind almonds in a food processor or blender. Cut creamy mixture into pieces about 2 inches square. Coat each square in ground almonds. Beat whole egg and egg white together. Dip nut-coated cream into egg mixture, then into cookie crumbs. Refrigerate at least 2 hours. Place several pieces into raised fryer basket. Lower into hot oil and fry 2 to 2½ minutes or until golden. Drain on paper towels and serve immediately. Makes 8 servings.

Churros, above; Fried Cream, above.

Batters & Sauces

For your convenience, each recipe in this book is complete, with the proper coating or batter and sauce if a specific one is required. In addition, I have included extra fritter batters in this section in case you want to experiment and develop recipes of your own. Use fresh fruits or vegetables from your garden and meats or fish that are special favorites with your family. Some of these are fairly standard batters, while others have a special flavor or texture, such as Beer Fritter Batter, page 146, or Yeast Fritter Batter, page 145.

Beer Fritter Batter creates a very light crispy coating that's good on vegetables or fish. Yeast Fritter Batter is similar, but slightly thicker than most batters. Although it takes longer to make, it is well worth the extra time because of the different yeast flavor and the light texture. Remember to have the food dry before coating with the batter.

Sauces are included with the appropriate recipes in other sections of the book. However, there are a number of sauces that are optional or a matter of personal preference. For example, some people like to squeeze lemon wedges over fish, while others prefer some type of prepared sauce. I have included several kinds of sauces that are compatible with fish and seafood. If you enjoy sauces on fried fish, you'll like the Creamy Cucumber-Dill Sauce, page 149, or Horseradish Yogurt Sauce, page 150. For those who like a more traditional accompaniment to fried fish, use the ever-popular Tartar Sauce, page 148, or Easy Seafood Sauce, page 148, which is a seafood cocktail sauce.

For fresh or frozen vegetables that are coated with crumbs or encased in a batter, Sour Cream Sauce, page 149, and Creole Sauce, page 150, are good choices. Each is different in flavor and texture, but equally good over a variety of vegetables.

Most fruit fritters don't actually need a sauce if they are generously sprinkle with powdered sugar or served with honey or maple syrup. If you are a sauce fan, be sure to sample the Maple-Pecan Sauce, page 151, or Apricot-Orange Sauce, page 151, on your fritters.

Yeast Fritter Batter

A thicker batter. Try it for fish, fillets, shrimp, carrot slices, zucchini sticks, eggplant wedges and green bell pepper rings.

1 (¼-oz.) pkg. active dry yeast
   (1 tablespoon)
½ teaspoon sugar
¼ cup warm water
½ teaspoon salt

1½ cups all-purpose flour
1 cup warm water
Vegetable oil for frying
Fish or vegetables

■■■■■■■ In a small bowl, sprinkle yeast and sugar in ¼ cup warm water. Let stand until yeast begins to foam, about 8 to 10 minutes. In a medium bowl, combine salt, flour, 1 cup warm water and yeast mixture. Beat with a spoon until lumps disappear. Cover and let rise until doubled in bulk, about 1½ to 2 hours. Stir down. Dip prepared fish or vegetables into batter. Place fryer basket in lowered position. Fry in hot oil until golden brown. Drain and serve warm. Makes about 3 cups batter, enough for 5 to 6 servings.

Fruit Fritter Batter

Try this wine batter with your favorite fruits.

1¼ cups all-purpose flour
1 cup white wine
1 tablespoon sugar
1 teaspoon grated lemon peel
¼ teaspoon salt

1 egg white
2 to 3 cups peeled sliced apples, pears
   or bananas
Sifted powdered sugar
Vegetable oil for frying

■■■■■■■ In a medium bowl, combine flour, wine, sugar, grated lemon peel and salt. Beat until smooth. Cover and refrigerate several hours. Just before using, beat egg white in a small bowl until stiff but not dry. Fold egg white into chilled batter. Pat sliced fruit dry with paper towels. Sprinkle fruit with powdered sugar. Dip fruit into chilled fritter batter. Place fryer basket in lowered position. Fry in hot oil until golden brown. Drain and sprinkle with more powdered sugar. Makes enough batter for 6 servings.

Beer Fritter Batter

A light, crispy batter for vegetables or fish. Especially good with onions, zucchini or clams.

1 cup all-purpose flour
¼ teaspoon salt
1 cup flat beer
2 tablespoons vegetable oil

2 egg whites
Vegetables or fish
Vegetable oil for frying

In a medium bowl, combine flour and salt. Make a well in center; pour in beer and oil. Beat with a rotary beater until smooth. Let stand at least 1 hour. In a small bowl, beat egg whites until stiff. Stir beer batter and fold in beaten egg whites. Dip prepared vegetables or fish into batter; let excess drip into bowl. Place fryer basket in lowered position. Fry in hot oil until golden brown. Drain and serve warm. Makes about 2 cups batter, enough for 4 servings.

Quick Vegetable Fritter Batter

Make this all-purpose batter at a moment's notice!

¾ cup all-purpose flour
1 teaspoon baking powder
½ teaspoon salt
¾ cup milk

1 egg, slightly beaten
Vegetables
Vegetable oil for frying

In a small bowl, combine flour, baking powder and salt. Gradually add milk, then egg. Beat until smooth. Dip prepared vegetables into batter. Place fryer basket in lowered position. Fry in hot oil until golden brown. Drain and serve warm. Makes about 2 cups batter, enough for 4 servings.

Tempura Batter

Use batter as soon as it is mixed because the ice water helps to create the special lacy effect when coated foods are fried.

1 egg yolk
2 cups ice water
⅛ teaspoon baking soda

1⅔ cups all-purpose flour
Shrimp or vegetables
Vegetable oil for frying

████████ In a medium bowl, combine egg yolk, ice water and baking soda. Stir in flour. Mix well with a wooden spoon. Dip shrimp or vegetables into batter. Place fryer basket in lowered position. Fry in hot oil until golden. Drain and serve warm. Makes about 4 cups batter, enough for 6 servings.

Quick Chinese-Plum Sauce

Serve warm over fried shrimp, ribs or won ton.

½ cup chutney
1 cup plum preserves

1 tablespoon wine vinegar
1 tablespoon brown sugar

████████ Chop large pieces of chutney. In a small saucepan, combine chutney, plum preserves, wine vinegar and brown sugar. Heat to boiling. Makes 1½ cups sauce.

Oriental Sweet-Sour Sauce

Serve hot over fried fish, chicken or pork.

2 tablespoons vegetable oil
1 clove garlic, crushed
2 carrots, thinly sliced
1 cup chicken broth or bouillon
½ cup sugar
½ cup red-wine vinegar

2 teaspoons soy sauce
2 tablespoons cornstarch
¼ cup water
1 cup fresh Chinese snow peas,
   if desired

████████ In a large skillet, heat oil and garlic. Add carrots. Stir-fry several minutes. Stir in chicken broth or bouillon, sugar, wine vinegar and soy sauce. Dissolve cornstarch in water. Add to mixture in skillet. Cook over low heat, stirring constantly, until thick and translucent. Add snow peas, if desired. Makes about 3 cups sauce.

Tartar Sauce

Serve with fried fish, shrimp or scallops.

½ cup mayonnaise
¼ cup sweet-pickle relish, well-drained
1 teaspoon instant minced onion

½ teaspoon Worcestershire sauce
1 teaspoon minced parsley

███████████ In a small bowl, combine mayonnaise, pickle relish, onion, Worcestershire sauce and parsley. Cover and refrigerate at least 1 hour to blend flavors. Makes ¾ cup sauce.

Easy Seafood Sauce

Serve with fried shrimp, scallops or other fried seafoods.

½ cup ketchup
1 tablespoon prepared horseradish
1 teaspoon Worcestershire sauce

1 teaspoon minced instant dry onion
1 teaspoon lemon juice

███████████ In a small bowl, combine ketchup, horseradish, Worcestershire sauce, onion and lemon juice. Cover and refrigerate at least 1 hour to blend flavors. Makes about ½ cup sauce.

Cheese Relish Sauce

Serve as a dip for Corn Dogs, page 74.

1 (10¾-oz.) can Cheddar cheese soup, undiluted

¼ cup sweet pickle relish
1 tablespoon prepared mustard

███████████ In a small saucepan, combine soup, relish and mustard. Heat until bubbly. Makes about 1½ cups sauce.

Creamy Cucumber-Dill Sauce

Serve with fried fish or seafood.

1 small cucumber
½ cup dairy sour cream
¼ cup mayonnaise
½ teaspoon seasoned salt

1 teaspoon finely chopped green
 onions
1 teaspoon dried dill weed

▬▬▬▬▬ Peel cucumber, cut in half and scoop out and discard seeds. Coarsely grate cucumber and drain. In a small bowl, combine grated cucumber, sour cream, mayonnaise, seasoned salt, green onions and dill weed. Makes about 1¼ cups sauce.

Curried Peach Sauce

Serve warm over fried chicken.

2 tablespoons butter
1½ tablespoons all-purpose flour
2 tablespoons brown sugar

2 tablespoons curry powder
¼ teaspoon salt
1 (16-oz.) can sliced peaches with syrup

▬▬▬▬▬ In a small saucepan, melt butter. Stir in flour, brown sugar, curry powder and salt. Drain peaches and pour syrup into curry mixture. Cook, stirring constantly, several minutes until mixture thickens. Add peaches with syrup. Makes about 2 cups sauce.

Sour Cream Sauce

Serve over veal or fried vegetables.

2 tablespoons all-purpose flour
2 tablespoons melted butter or
 margarine
¾ cup milk
1 teaspoon horseradish

¼ teaspoon salt
⅛ teaspoon pepper
½ teasoon Worcestershire sauce
½ cup sour cream

▬▬▬▬▬ In a small saucepan, stir flour into butter or margarine. Stir in milk, then horseradish, salt, pepper and Worcestershire sauce. Cook, stirring constantly, over low heat until slightly thickened. Remove from heat; stir in sour cream. Makes about 1 cup sauce.

Horseradish Yogurt Sauce

Serve with fried fish or shrimp.

1 cup plain yogurt
2 tablespoons prepared horseradish
¼ cup sliced green onions

1 teaspoon dry mustard
¼ teaspoon salt

━━━━━━━━ In a small bowl, combine yogurt, horseradish, green onions, dry mustard and salt. Cover and refrigerate at least 1 hour to blend flavors. Makes about 1 cup sauce.

Quick Horseradish-Dill Sauce

Serve with fried fish or scallops.

⅓ cup mayonnaise
¼ cup minced dill pickle

1 tablespoon horseradish

━━━━━━━━ In a small bowl, combine mayonnaise, pickle and horseradish. Makes about ⅔ cup sauce.

Creole Sauce

Serve warm over fried okra, eggplant or zucchini.

2 tablespoons butter or margarine
½ cup chopped onion
¼ cup chopped green bell pepper
¼ cup chopped celery
1 medium tomato, peeled, chopped

1 (8-oz.) can tomato sauce
1 (3-oz.) can sliced mushrooms, drained
¼ teaspoon salt
⅛ teaspoon garlic salt

━━━━━━━━ In a medium saucepan, melt butter or margarine. Add onion, bell pepper, celery and tomato. Cover and simmer until vegetables are tender. Stir in tomato sauce, mushrooms, salt and garlic salt. Cook another 2 to 3 minutes. Makes about 2 cups sauce.

Apricot-Orange Sauce

Serve over banana, date or pineaple fritters.

1 cup dried apricots
1¾ cups water
¼ cup sugar

1 tablespoon orange-flavored liqueur
3 to 4 drops almond extract

━━━━━━━━━ In a small heavy saucepan, combine apricots, water and sugar. Bring to a boil; cover and simmer 1 hour. Remove from heat. Add liqueur and almond extract. In a food processor or blender, process sauce to a puree. Makes about 1 cup sauce.

Special Orange Sauce

Serve warm over banana or blueberry fritters, or fig or date won ton.

1 cup orange marmalade
⅓ cup orange-flavored liqueur

2 tablespoons lemon juice

━━━━━━━━━ In a small saucepan, combine marmalade, liqueur and lemon juice. Heat until marmalade melts. Makes about 1⅓ cups sauce.

Maple-Pecan Sauce

Serve with Traditional Banana Fritters or any other fruit fritters.

¼ cup butter or margarine
½ cup powdered sugar
2 tablespoons maple syrup

¼ cup water
½ cup finely chopped pecans

━━━━━━━━━ In a small saucepan, heat butter or margarine until light brown. Cool slightly. Gradually mix in powdered sugar. Stir in maple syrup and water. Bring to a boil; simmer 1 minute. Remove from heat. Stir in nuts. Serve warm. Makes 1 cup sauce.

Hot Pots & Meat Fondues

Hot Pot, borrowed from oriental cooking, is usually a large metal pot filled with broth or oil and surrounded by uncooked meats, fish and vegetables. Cooking is done at the table with each person cooking his own selections.

Your deep-fryer can be used the same way. Place it on a level heat-resistant trivet. Heat broth or oil in deep-fryer according to manufacturer's directions. Arrange sliced vegetables and meats or fish on a platter near the deep-fryer. Then let each person pick up his own food with a fondue fork and cook it in the deep-fryer. You can also use the fryer basket. It is perfect for four to six servings.

The thermostatic control in a deep-fryer keeps the temperature of the broth or oil just about right for frying small pieces of flank or sirloin steak. Usually tender cuts of meat such as beef sirloin or tenderloin are used for this kind of recipe. However, marinated flank steak, sliced very thin, is a nice change. Before frying these meats. pat dry with paper towels to avoid spattering.

Meat and vegetables cooked in broth provide a flavor surprise. When all the meats and vegetables are cooked, unplug your deep-fryer and let it cool slightly. Using a soup ladle, dip out the broth into soup mugs or bowls for each person. It's delicious!

Beef Hot Pot, page 155.

Fondued Flank Steak

Marinade provides a hint of oriental flavor.

1 lb. flank steak, cut across grain
   ⅜-inch thick
1 cup beef bouillon
⅓ cup sherry wine

2 tablespoons soy sauce
1 clove garlic, crushed
⅛ teaspoon onion salt
Vegetable oil for frying

▬▬▬▬▬ Place meat in a shallow dish. In a small saucepan, combine bouillon, wine, soy sauce, garlic and onion salt. Simmer uncovered 5 minutes. Cool and pour bouillon mixture over meat. Cover and refrigerate several hours or overnight. Drain meat and pat dry with paper towels. Place several pieces in raised fryer basket. Lower into hot oil and fry 1 to 2 minutes or until meat is desired degree of doneness. Drain and serve hot. Makes 4 servings.

Chicken-Vegetable Hot Pot

A complete meal in a pot!

2 cans condensed chicken broth
2 cups water
1 lb. boneless chicken breast, cut up in
   small pieces

2 medium zucchini, sliced
4 cups fresh spinach leaves
½ lb. fresh mushrooms, sliced
Soy sauce

▬▬▬▬▬ Pour chicken broth and water into unheated deep-fryer. Heat 8 minutes. Drop in chicken pieces and zucchini. Cook 3 to 4 minutes. Add spinach and mushrooms. Cook another 3 to 4 minutes or until done. Spoon out chicken and vegetables, then broth. Serve hot with soy sauce. Makes 4 servings.

Skewered-Steak Fondue

Cook at the table in your deep-fryer.

1 lb. fillet of beef or boneless sirloin
1 cup soy sauce
½ cup dry white wine
2 tablespoons vegetable oil

2 cloves garlic, minced
1 teaspoon ground ginger
24 to 30 small fresh mushrooms
Vegetable oil for frying

▬▬▬▬▬ Slice beef in ⅛-inch-thick strips and place in a shallow dish. In a medium bowl, combine soy sauce, white wine, 2 tablespoons oil, garlic and ginger. Pour over meat. Cover and refrigerate several hours or overnight. Drain meat. Pat dry with paper towels. Arrange strips of beef on 4 skewers alternately with mushrooms. Place 2 skewers in raised fryer basket. Lower into hot oil and fry ½ to 1 minute or until meat is desired degree of doneness. Drain and serve hot. Makes 4 servings.

Beef Hot Pot

A great idea borrowed from oriental gourmets. (Photo on page 153.)

1 to 1½ lbs. boneless beef sirloin or
   tenderloin, partially frozen
8 green onions
2 to 4 summer squash, crookneck or
   zucchini

12 to 16 mushrooms
4 broccoli stalks
4 (10½-oz.) cans condensed beef broth
   or bouillon

Teriyaki Sauce:
⅔ cup soy sauce
2 tablespoons lemon juice
2 tablespoons honey

½ teaspoon ground ginger
½ teaspoon garlic salt

▬▬▬▬▬ Prepare Teriyaki Sauce. Cut partially frozen beef in very thin slices. Cut green onions in 2-inch lengths. Thinly slice squash and mushrooms. Break apart broccoli flowerets in small clusters and thinly slice stalks. Arrange meat and prepared vegetables on a tray. Place fryer basket in lowered position. Pour broth or bouillon into unheated deep-fryer. Bring broth or bouillon to a boil. Carefully drop in a small amount of green onions, squash, and broccoli; simmer about 1 minute. Add a small amount of meat and a few mushrooms. Cook to desired doneness, another 1 to 2 minutes. Raise basket and remove food, or use an oriental strainer to scoop out cooked food. Repeat process until meat and vegetables are all cooked. Dip meat and vegetables into Teriyaki Sauce. Unplug deep-fryer. Carefully ladle remaining broth into mugs or soup bowls and serve hot. Makes 4 to 6 servings.

Teriyaki Sauce:
In a small bowl, combine soy sauce, lemon juice, honey, ginger and garlic salt. Stir to blend well.

Bali Hai Steak Fondue

A taste of the tropics! You'll need skewers for this one.

½ cup vegetable oil
½ cup dry red wine
2 tablespoons ketchup
2 tablespoons molasses
2 tablespoons minced crystallized
   ginger
½ teaspoon salt

1 clove garlic, minced
½ teaspoon pepper
½ teasoon curry powder
1 lb. boneless top sirloin steak
Vegetable oil for frying
2 cups cooked buttered rice

▬▬▬▬▬ In a small bowl, combine ½ cup oil, wine, ketchup, molasses, crystallized ginger, salt, garlic, pepper and curry. Cut steak in very thin crosswise strips. Pour marinade over meat. Cover and refrigerate 2 hours. Drain well and pat dry with paper towels. Thread meat onto 4 skewers in accordion fashion. Place 2 skewers into raised fryer basket. Lower into hot oil and fry 1 to 2½ minutes or until meat is desired degree of doneness. Drain and serve over hot buttered rice. Makes 4 servings.

Spicy Beef Fondue

It's fun to cook this beef at the table.

3 cups chicken broth or bouillon
1 cup white wine
2 onions, thinly sliced
2 celery stalks, sliced
2 cloves garlic, minced
12 peppercorns
1 teaspoon salt

1 teaspoon dried tarragon leaves
4 sprigs fresh parsley
2 bay leaves
2 lbs. boneless beef sirloin or tenderloin, cut in 1-inch cubes
Steak sauce, if desired

▬▬▬▬▬▬ The day before serving, in deep-fryer combine broth or bouillon, wine, onion, celery, garlic, peppercorns, salt, tarragon, parsley sprigs and bay leaves. Bring to a boil. Cool and pour into a bowl or plastic container. Cover and refrigerate overnight. Before reheating, strain mixture through a fine sieve. Pour strained broth into deep-fryer. Bring to a boil. Use fondue forks or skewers to spear cubes of meat. Dip meat into hot broth. Cook 30 to 60 seconds or until meat is desired degree of doneness. Serve plain or with steak sauce, if desired. Makes 4 to 6 servings.

Hot Pot

A mini-version of the authentic Chinese hot pot.

10 to 12 uncooked medium shrimp
1 whole boneless skinned chicken
   breast, halved
3 cups chicken broth or bouillon
1 cup coarsely chopped Chinese
   cabbage

½ cup sliced celery
2 green onions, cut in 1-inch pieces
6 to 8 canned water chestnuts, sliced
Soy sauce or teriyaki sauce

▬▬▬▬▬▬ Peel and devein shrimp. Cut chicken in thin slivers. Arrange shrimp and chicken on a tray with prepared vegetables. Place fryer basket in lowered position. Pour broth or bouillon into unheated deep-fryer. Heat broth or bouillon to boiling. Carefully drop in small amounts of shrimp, chicken, Chinese cabbage and celery. Simmer about 1 minute. Add a small amount of green onions and water chestnuts. Cook several minutes to desired doneness. Raise basket and remove food or use an oriental strainer to scoop out cooked food. Repeat process until all shrimp, chicken and vegetables are cooked. Dip into soy sauce or teriyaki sauce. Unplug deep-fryer. Carefully ladle remaining broth into mugs and serve hot. Makes 4 servings.

Heat vegetables, wine and herbs with chicken broth or bouillon. Cool, pour into a bowl or plastic container, cover and refrigerate overnight.

How to Make Spicy Beef Fondue

Strain broth-and-vegetable mixture just before reheating.

Let each person cook his own meat in seasoned broth in deep-fryer, using fondue forks or skewers.

INDEX